READINGS ON

OF MICE AND MEN

OTHER TITLES IN THE GREENHAVEN PRESS LITERARY COMPANION SERIES:

AMERICAN AUTHORS

Maya Angelou
Stephen Crane
Emily Dickinson
William Faulkner
F. Scott Fitzgerald
Nathaniel Hawthorne
Ernest Hemingway
Herman Melville
Arthur Miller
Eugene O'Neill
Edgar Allan Poe
John Steinbeck
Mark Twain

BRITISH AUTHORS

Jane Austen
Joseph Conrad
Charles Dickens

WORLD AUTHORS

Fyodor Dostoyevsky
Homer
Sophocles

AMERICAN LITERATURE

The Great Gatsby
The Scarlet Letter

BRITISH LITERATURE

Animal Farm
The Canterbury Tales
Lord of the Flies
Romeo and Juliet
Shakespeare: The Comedies
Shakespeare: The Sonnets
Shakespeare: The Tragedies
A Tale of Two Cities

WORLD LITERATURE

Diary of a Young Girl

THE GREENHAVEN PRESS
Literary Companion
TO AMERICAN LITERATURE

READINGS ON

OF MICE AND MEN

David Bender, *Publisher*
Bruno Leone, *Executive Editor*
Brenda Stalcup, *Managing Editor*
Bonnie Szumski, *Series Editor*
Jill Karson, *Book Editor*

Greenhaven Press, San Diego, CA

Library of Congress Cataloging-in-Publication Data

Readings on Of mice and men / Jill Karson, book editor.
    p.   cm. — (The Greenhaven Press literary
companion to American literature)
    Includes bibliographical references and index.
    ISBN 1-56510-653-9 (lib. bdg. : alk. paper). —
ISBN 1-56510-652-0 (pbk. : alk. paper)
    1. Steinbeck, John, 1902–1968. Of mice and men. 2.
Salinas River Valley (Calif.)—In literature. 3. Friendship
in literature. 4. Cowboys in literature. I. Karson, Jill.
II. Series.
PS3537.T32340468   1998
813'.52—dc21   97-10484
                                            CIP

Every effort has been made to trace the owners of copyrighted material. The articles in this volume may have been edited for content, length, and/or reading level. The titles have been changed to enhance the editorial purpose of the Opposing Viewpoints® concept. Those interested in locating the original source will find the complete citation on the first page of each article.

Cover photo: Photofest

Copyright ©1998 by Greenhaven Press, Inc.
PO Box 289009
San Diego, CA 92198-9009
Printed in the U.S.A.

> **"A study of the dreams and pleasures of everyone in the world."**
>
> *John Steinbeck,*
> *commenting on*
> **Of Mice and Men**

CONTENTS

FOREWORD

*"'Tis the good reader that
makes the good book."*

Ralph Waldo Emerson

The story's bare facts are simple: The captain, an old and scarred seafarer, walks with a peg leg made of whale ivory. He relentlessly drives his crew to hunt the world's oceans for the great white whale that crippled him. After a long search, the ship encounters the whale and a fierce battle ensues. Finally the captain drives his harpoon into the whale, but the harpoon line catches the captain about the neck and drags him to his death.

A simple story, a straightforward plot—yet, since the 1851 publication of Herman Melville's *Moby-Dick*, readers and critics have found many meanings in the struggle between Captain Ahab and the whale. To some, the novel is a cautionary tale that depicts how Ahab's obsession with revenge leads to his insanity and death. Others believe that the whale represents the unknowable secrets of the universe and that Ahab is a tragic hero who dares to challenge fate by attempting to discover this knowledge. Perhaps Melville intended Ahab as a criticism of Americans' tendency to become involved in well-intentioned but irrational causes. Or did Melville model Ahab after himself, letting his fictional character express his anger at what he perceived as a cruel and distant god?

Although literary critics disagree over the meaning of *Moby-Dick*, readers do not need to choose one particular interpretation in order to gain an understanding of Melville's novel. Instead, by examining various analyses, they can gain numerous insights into the issues that lie under the surface of the basic plot. Studying the writings of literary critics can also aid readers in making their own assessments of *Moby-Dick* and other literary works and in developing analytical thinking skills.

The Greenhaven Literary Companion Series was created with these goals in mind. Designed for young adults, this unique anthology series provides an engaging and comprehensive introduction to literary analysis and criticism. The essays included in the Literary Companion Series are chosen for their accessibility to a young adult audience and are expertly edited in consideration of both the reading and comprehension levels of this audience. In addition, each essay is introduced by a concise summation that presents the contributing writer's main themes and insights. Every anthology in the Literary Companion Series contains a varied selection of critical essays that cover a wide time span and express diverse views. Wherever possible, primary sources are represented through excerpts from authors' notebooks, letters, and journals and through contemporary criticism.

Each title in the Literary Companion Series pays careful consideration to the historical context of the particular author or literary work. In-depth biographies and detailed chronologies reveal important aspects of authors' lives and emphasize the historical events and social milieu that influenced their writings. To facilitate further research, every anthology includes primary and secondary source bibliographies of articles and/or books selected for their suitability for young adults. These engaging features make the Greenhaven Literary Companion Series ideal for introducing students to literary analysis in the classroom or as a library resource for young adults researching the world's great authors and literature.

Exceptional in its focus on young adults, the Greenhaven Literary Companion Series strives to present literary criticism in a compelling and accessible format. Every title in the series is intended to spark readers' interest in leading American and world authors, to help them broaden their understanding of literature, and to encourage them to formulate their own analyses of the literary works that they read. It is the editors' hope that young adult readers will find these anthologies to be true companions in their study of literature.

INTRODUCTION

Although *The Grapes of Wrath* is widely considered John Steinbeck's masterpiece, *Of Mice and Men* is perhaps his most durable work. The novel offers an illuminating glimpse into the lives of migrant farmworkers of the 1930s, yet it is much more than a fictionalized chronicle of farm labor. Rather, it transcends its historical context and strikes a timeless, universal chord in readers of all ages because it appeals to basic human desires. Readers recognize the bond of friendship between the two main characters, Lennie and George, their dream of security, and their longing for a place to call home.

Perhaps the most striking feature of commentary on *Of Mice and Men* is the wide divergence of critical opinion. Indeed, the essays in this volume testify to the surprising diversity of views penned by Steinbeck critics since the book's publication in 1937. Some critics call the novel a classic tragedy; others argue very strongly that it is not. Some believe that *Of Mice and Men* is a political vehicle for Steinbeck's commentary on a social system that beats down the underdog; another contends that personal flaws account for the protagonists' downfall. One labels *Of Mice and Men* a critique of society's injustice to women; another emphasizes the book's mythic overtones. As critics continue to offer various interpretations of *Of Mice and Men*, it is safe to say that Steinbeck's enormous gift for storytelling will continue to engage readers and fuel thought-provoking debate.

To aid the reader of Steinbeck's *Of Mice and Men*, this volume gathers nineteen essays from a broad range of critics. The selections are chosen for their readability and provide a wide variety of information and opinion about *Of Mice and Men*. Some, such as Burton Rascoe's 1938 essay, which praises Steinbeck's skill as a narrator, are considered classic studies of the work. Others offer interesting, newer interpretations of the novel, such as Leland Person's essay, which identifies an "alternate manhood" in the novel. In addition, because *Of Mice and Men* is so closely connected to drama—the book was written as a play/novella—a chapter is devoted to critiques of the play version.

Several features make *Readings on* Of Mice and Men easy to use. Each essay's introduction clearly summarizes the author's main ideas. A biography provides important information about John Steinbeck and lends historical background to *Of Mice and Men.* A chronology places the work in a broader historical context. Additional tools include an annotated table of contents, a thorough index, and a bibliography. Together, these features make research accessible, interesting, and informative.

John Steinbeck: A Biography

John Steinbeck was born and raised in the Salinas Valley of west-central California. Any serious discussion of his life and work must begin here, for this fertile, beautiful California valley—extending from the Monterey Bay in the north to San Luis Obispo in the south and stretching between the ranges of the Santa Lucia and Gabilan mountains—exerted a powerful influence on the man and the writer. From this landscape of rolling hills, rugged mountains, and majestic shorelines, Steinbeck drew material for the settings, characters, and incidents of his most memorable books. Indeed, few American authors have so thoroughly mined the riches of their homeland. It is no accident, then, that so much of his fiction takes place in California, specifically in the long valley that he deeply loved, chronicled, and called home.

The California into which John Ernst Steinbeck Jr. was born on February 27, 1902, promised excitement and opportunity. Still reminiscent of its colorful frontier history and bustling gold rush days, California at the turn of the century enjoyed a healthy economy and rapid development, and an enterprising middle class was taking root. Although his parents, John Ernst Steinbeck and Olive Hamilton Steinbeck, were far from wealthy, they lived in a large, comfortable Victorian house and were socially and culturally active. The family included young John's elder sisters, ten-year-old Esther and eight-year-old Elizabeth. John's father managed a flour mill and later opened a feed-and-grain store. When the latter enterprise failed, the elder Steinbeck became an accountant.

REARING AN INTELLECTUAL

The Steinbeck home nurtured young John's budding intellect. The house was filled with books and the family read aloud to each other as entertainment. John's mother, Olive, held considerable ambitions for her only boy. Wishing to produce a cultured and educated son, she took charge of his education at an early age. To the small boy she read the classics of world literature, including the Bible when he was three, and *Robin Hood* and *Treasure Island* when he was four. Perhaps most importantly, his mother's own inquisitive nature kindled Steinbeck's imagination and capacity for wonder. As Steinbeck biographer Jackson J. Benson points out:

> It was she who planted the seed with her bedroom stories of enchanted forests, she who encouraged her son to use his imagination, to discover a world made up of both the seen and the unseen, and to perceive the nature of things intuitively and poetically, and not only by the common sense that alone was valued in the masculine society of a "frontier town."

Undoubtedly, John's mother had a great impact on John's development, but it was Steinbeck's father, not his mother, who supported his writing endeavors. In later years, Steinbeck recalled:

> In my struggle to be a writer, it was he who supported and backed me and explained me—not my mother. She wanted me desperately to be something decent like a banker. She would have liked me to be a successful writer like Tarkington but this she didn't believe I could do. But my father wanted me to be myself.... And I think he liked the complete ruthlessness of my design to be a writer in spite of mother and hell.

Steinbeck described his father as a somewhat withdrawn man, frustrated by his lack of success in business yet also strong, gentle, and sensitive. As one of Steinbeck's sisters commented about the elder Steinbeck, "He suffered for people in their trouble," perhaps accounting, in part, for Steinbeck's great humanity, his compassion for the misfits and outcasts of life.

When John was nine, he received a gift that profoundly influenced his view of language and literature:

> One day, an aunt gave me a book and fatuously ignored my resentment. I stared at the black print with hatred, and then gradually the pages opened and let me in. The magic happened. The Bible and Shakespeare and *Pilgrim's Progress* belonged to everyone. But this was mine—secretly mine. It was a cut version of the Caxton "Morte d'Arthur" of Thomas Malory. I loved the old spellings of the words—and the words no longer used. Perhaps a passionate love for the English language opened to me from this one book. I was delighted to find out paradoxes—that "cleave" means both to stick together and to cut apart.... For a long time, I had a secret language.

John read *Le Morte Darthur* with Mary, his younger sister born in 1909. Armed with their "secret language"—and fertile imaginations—the two would escape to the hills and play out the romantic adventures of King Arthur. Steinbeck's interest in Malory proved to be lifelong; years later, Arthurian themes would make their way into some of Steinbeck's most well read fiction.

John entered Salinas High School in 1915. He was somewhat of a social failure. Shy and withdrawn, he was not particularly good-looking or athletic, had no close friends, and eschewed most social activities. Academically, he was an unremarkable student, but he excelled in English and eventually became editor of the school yearbook, in which his first published work appeared. These early forays in yearbook writing clearly show young Steinbeck's emerging wit: "The English room, which is just down the hall from the office, is the sanctuary of Shakespeare, the temple of Milton and Byron, and the terror of Freshmen. English is a kind of high brow idea of the American language. A hard job is made of nothing at all and nothing at all is made of a hard job. It is in this room and this room alone that the English language is spoken." By the end of his freshman year, Steinbeck had set his sights on becoming a writer.

THE RELUCTANT SCHOLAR

Steinbeck's success in high school English and his ambition to write prompted him to begin his studies at Stanford University as an English major in the fall of 1919. His college career proved intermittent and erratic; he attended classes off and on for six years and never earned a degree. While his performance at the university was for the most part mediocre, several important events in this period left their mark on Steinbeck. First, he took a writing course under the talented but demanding Edith Ronald Mirrielees. The strict professor liked Steinbeck's writing—she thought his work should be published—but challenged him to pare excess words and ornamentation. At first, Steinbeck did not take this criticism well: He loved words and wanted to exercise his vocabulary through his writing. Eventually, however, Mirrielees won him over and he worked to develop a more disciplined prose style. About her demand for conciseness, Steinbeck said in a letter to a friend, "She does one thing for you. She makes you get over what you want to say." Under her tutelage, Steinbeck honed his writing skills, creating the lean, terse narrative style that would later earn him praise.

Also of major significance was workingman experience gained during Steinbeck's frequent hiatuses from Stanford that not only influenced his worldview but also directly planted the seed that would become *Of Mice and Men.* Steinbeck spent his time away from school working for wages on road gangs and commercial farms, notably on the sprawling Spreckels Sugar Ranch. "I was a bindle-stiff myself for quite a spell. I worked in the same country that [*Of Mice and Men*] is laid in," Steinbeck told reporters after the publication of his novel years later. The Spreckels Sugar Ranch was actually a number of ranches dotting the land from King City in the south to Santa Clara in the north. Spreckels grew sugar beets primarily, but also raised alfalfa and hay as well as some cattle. Its huge beet crop was planted and harvested by hired hands—bindle stiffs, or hobos, and migrants—who traveled to whichever Spreckels ranch had work and stayed as long as their labor was needed. George and Lennie in *Of Mice and Men* are bindle stiffs who find work on a ranch just south of Soledad.

To understand the impact this job had on Steinbeck, it is important to note that Steinbeck came of age during a time when California's booming agricultural industry was plagued by labor problems. Commercial growers relied on cheap, seasonal labor, often taking advantage of the flood of migrant workers who roamed the west, looking for work. Many were of Mexican, Japanese, or Filipino descent. Their lives were marked by poverty and few enjoyed more than the most meager living conditions. Although the farm industry was undergoing a historic transformation—the advent of high-tech farm equipment rendered many workers obsolete—for a time in the 1920s Steinbeck became part of this working culture.

STUDENT-TURNED-WORKINGMAN

At Spreckels, Steinbeck lived in the bunkhouses and held a variety of jobs including carpenter's helper and bench chemist, a job which required him to run tests on the beet harvests. The shop foreman who at one time supervised Steinbeck commented on his irritating habit of disappearing from his work station and retreating to some remote corner where he would scribble notes to himself, most likely recording his impressions of ranch life. Steinbeck's observations proved a rich source of writing material. Back in school, the university literary magazine, *Stanford Spectator,* published Steinbeck's story about a ranch crew, something of a precursor to *Of Mice and Men*:

> A coal fire roared in the bunkhouse of the foreign camp. The Filipinos sat on the floor with their feet under them. From the outside the howling wind came through the cracks in the house and made the burlap hangings move restlessly. Burlap tacked loosely on the walls, a littered floor of dust colored wood, a few boxes to sit on, and the fat-bellied stove, that was the lounging room of the bunkhouse. Three of the pock-marked, brown men played cards on the floor under a coal oil lamp. They threw down their cards without a word. No one was talking in the room. Ten or twelve more of the squatty figures were dumped about the room, half smiling because there would be no work in the beet fields the next day.

His time at Spreckels not only gave Steinbeck valuable work experience, but also brought the impressionable young writer into direct contact with a kaleidoscope of characters, most from the lower echelon of society. Steinbeck got on well with his fellow workers despite their lower-class status. He regarded them with warmth and compassion and without condescension or mere pity. He was deeply moved by their struggles. Most importantly, he discovered that their basic human qualities—their needs and desires—were not so very different from the rest of mankind's, despite differences in race, origins, or social position. Steinbeck's compassion for these people would manifest itself years later in *Of Mice and Men*, as well as other novels.

PURSUING A WRITING CAREER

Not caring to fulfill the academic requirements for a degree, Steinbeck left Stanford for good in 1925. In June of that year he packed his bags and headed for Lake Tahoe, where he had been offered a job as a maintenance man. Unsure of his future but certain that he wanted to make his way as a writer, his goal was to earn enough money to travel to New York City. There, he believed, he could launch his writing career. By November he took a job on a freighter bound for New York. The sea voyage through the tropical waters of the Caribbean and the Panama Canal piqued Steinbeck's writer's instinct. Fascinated by the vivid scenery, Steinbeck would fictionalize his impressions in his first book, *Cup of Gold*.

After the exhilarating sea voyage, Steinbeck's arrival in New York was somewhat of a shock. He recalled in an article years later: "It horrified me. There was something monstrous about it—the tall buildings looming to the sky and the lights shining through the falling snow. I crept ashore—frightened and cold and with a touch of panic in my stomach." Yet Steinbeck was determined to see his work published, and he set to the task with alacrity and gusto. Writing stories on the side, he earned a living as a construction worker and later as a reporter at the *New York American,* where he found he did not enjoy news writing; its rigid parameters did not allow the creative expression that Steinbeck craved.

This was a grim time for Steinbeck. Not one of his stories was published, and he was terminated from his job at the newspaper. The only bright spot in Steinbeck's New York stay was one publisher's enthusiasm for one of Steinbeck's stories. Unfortunately, the story was never published. Bitterly disappointed and at the end of his rope, Steinbeck packed his rejected manuscripts and boarded a freighter headed for San Francisco.

REFUGE IN WRITING

Back in California, Steinbeck secured a job as the caretaker of a huge estate at Lake Tahoe, which he would call home for the next two years. Considering that Steinbeck often grappled with self-doubt and a fear of loneliness, his choice was curious: As the first snowstorm of the season descended upon Steinbeck's tiny cabin, he faced loneliness and isolation more powerful than any he had previously experienced. But paradoxically, the solitude of the Sierra Nevada—he was snowed in for eight months—lent itself well to Steinbeck's singular pursuit; with very few demands on his time, he finished many short stories and, by February 1928, the novel *Cup of Gold.* He sent the manuscript to former Stanford classmate Ted Miller in New York. Miller had promised to place Steinbeck's manuscripts with publishers, and in January 1929, Steinbeck received the happy news that McBride and Company would publish *Cup of Gold.* The reviews were tepid and the book was not widely read; nevertheless, its publication marked the onset of a happy and prolific decade in which Steinbeck would shine, both personally and professionally.

In Lake Tahoe, Steinbeck had fallen in love with a vacationing secretary named Carol Henning. The couple married in January 1930 and settled in Los Angeles. Carol recognized Steinbeck's talent and encouraged his writing endeavors. Marriage seemed to agree with Steinbeck, and the contented writer pursued his literary career with vigor. He wrote, and Carol typed and edited. About her invaluable assistance, Steinbeck wrote in a letter to a friend, "It's a dirty shame Carol has to work so hard. She's putting in nine hours a day at it. I wish I could do it but my typing is so very lousy." In another letter he proclaimed, "Carol is a good influence on my work. . . . I have the time and the energy and it gives me pleasure to work, and now I do not seem to have to fight as much reluctance to work as I used to have."

About this time, Steinbeck met marine biologist Ed Ricketts, who would prove to be the greatest single influence on Steinbeck's artistic development. To Steinbeck, Ricketts was a fascinating character. He was exceedingly well read in many areas. He had a reputation not only for his sharp, analytical mind, but also for his wry sense of humor. Like Steinbeck, Ricketts loved to talk, analyze, and philosophize. He could debate a wide range of topics, and he enjoyed playing devil's advocate. In short, he was the perfect companion for Steinbeck. The importance of their subsequent eighteen-year-friendship cannot be understated. Ricketts was Steinbeck's closest friend, mentor, and partner. His biological views suffuse much of Steinbeck's work. He even served as the model for some of Steinbeck's most memorable characters, including Doc in *Cannery Row*.

Satisfying personal relationships aside, Steinbeck was in the same trouble financially as the rest of the country. The stock market had crashed in 1929, a disaster that heralded severe economic hardship across the globe. Millions of workers were unemployed and businesses and banks were failing across the nation. Yet the Steinbecks were somewhat insulated from the effects of the Great Depression for several reasons, as Steinbeck recalled years later in an *Esquire* article:

> The Depression was no financial shock to me. I didn't have any money to lose, but in common with millions I did dislike hunger and cold. I had two assets. My father owned a tiny three-room cottage in Pacific Grove in California, and he let me live in it without rent. That was the first safety. Pacific Grove is on the sea. That was the second. People in inland cities or in the closed and shuttered industrial cemeteries had greater problems than I. Given the sea a man must be very stupid to starve. The great reservoir of food is always available. I took a large part of my protein food from the sea.

> I must drop the "I" for "we" now, for there was a fairly large group of us poor kids, all living alike. We pooled our troubles, our money when we had some, our inventiveness, and our pleasures. I remember it as a warm and friendly time. Only illness frightened us.

About the time he met Ricketts, Steinbeck was recommended to the literary agency of Mavis McIntosh and Elizabeth Otis, who took him on as a client in 1931. Their professional association would last throughout Steinbeck's career. When they met, Steinbeck was plodding through some frustrating projects: *Dissonant Harmony*, a novel that he never completed and about which not much is known, and *Murder at Full Moon*, a detective story that was never published. He was working intermittently on *To an Unknown God* and *Pastures of Heaven*, ten collected short stories about a family named Munroe. *Pastures of Heaven* was published in 1932; an encouraged Steinbeck returned to rewriting *To an Unknown God*, a historical saga of the Salinas Valley to which Steinbeck was so emotionally tied. At Ricketts's prompting, he changed the title to *To a God Unknown*. Meanwhile, *Pastures of Heaven* garnered bad reviews and sold so poorly that the book had to be remaindered before the publishers went bankrupt.

A Change in Fortune

"This has been a very bad year all around for us," Steinbeck wrote in a letter to college friend Carl Wilhelmson. Then, Steinbeck's mother suffered a stroke, rendering her a helpless invalid. John and Carol spent a great deal of time caring for both Olive and the grief-stricken elder Steinbeck. Despite financial hardship and family tragedy, however, several fortuitous events occurred during this time. In conversations with his father, Steinbeck conceived the idea for the collection of stories that would become *The Red Pony*, one of Steinbeck's most loved creations, featuring a boy who is given a colt. He also became interested in a work about poor Mexicans called *paisans*. Their story, *Tortilla Flat*, would skyrocket Steinbeck to fame.

In the meantime, Steinbeck was refining *To a God Unknown*. The book was published in 1933. The same year, the *North American Review* published two of the pony stories. In 1934 the *North American Review* published the short story "The Murder," for which Steinbeck won the O. Henry Award for the best story of the year. At last, Steinbeck was enjoying literary acceptance, and his happiness was overshadowed only by his mother's death in 1934.

NATIONAL RECOGNITION

Ironically, Steinbeck was having a rough time getting *Tortilla Flat* published. The novel that would eventually land on the best-seller list was rejected by five publishers. Steinbeck's fortune changed, however, in January 1935, when he was contacted by New York publisher Pascal Covici, who had read and liked *Pastures of Heaven.* Covici offered to not only publish *Tortilla Flat* but also reissue Steinbeck's earlier books. *Tortilla Flat* hit the bookstands in May 1935. It was an immediate success. The bittersweet story follows a group of free-spirited *paisanos* who had been likened to Arthurian knights. Readers not only appreciated the droll humor but also were deeply moved by the pathos of the comic characters. Sadly, Steinbeck's father did not live to see the public's reaction to *Tortilla Flat*; the elder Steinbeck died a few days before the book was released.

With *Tortilla Flat* Steinbeck finally received recognition as a literary artist. Although Steinbeck disliked being a public figure, he was happy with the book's success and enthused about his next project, a story of two Marxists who attempt to organize an agricultural strike. The book's subject matter paralleled the labor movement sweeping the nation's agricultural regions—and the attempts to repress it. Steinbeck's book, titled *In Dubious Battle*, was released in 1936 and sold moderately well.

OF MICE AND MEN

Throughout his life, Steinbeck suffered misgivings about his literary ability and shunned being a public figure. Fighting the demands of celebrity, Steinbeck and his wife bought a piece of land on the outskirts of Los Gatos, a quiet community just north of Monterey. As Carol oversaw the building of a house, John began working on a new novel, tentatively titled *Something That Happened.* The story traced life among the hired hands of a Salinas Valley ranch. Undoubtedly, the story was strongly influenced by Steinbeck's college-age experiences as a laborer on the Spreckels Sugar Ranch.

As Steinbeck wrote, the urge to try a new writing technique grew. He decided to structure his novel like a play. As he wrote to a friend, Wilbur Needham, in May 1936: "I'm going into training to write for the theatre which seems to be waking up. I have some ideas for a new dramatic form which I'm experimenting with. Of course I don't know yet whether I am capable of writing for the theater. Just have to learn."

Steinbeck finished a manuscript quickly, but at the end of May he had a "minor tragedy," which he humorously recounted to Elizabeth Otis:

> Minor tragedy stalked. My setter pup left alone one night, made confetti of about half of my ms. book. Two months work to do over again. It sets me back. There was no other draft. I was pretty mad but the poor little fellow may have been acting critically. I didn't want to ruin a good dog for a ms. I'm not sure is good at all. He only got an ordinary spanking with his punishment flyswatter. But there's the work to do over from the start.

He continued working on the novel, but under a new title suggested by Ed Ricketts, *Of Mice and Men*, from the Robert Burns poem that captures the essence of Ricketts's naturalistic philosophy that man is a victim of forces he cannot control.

> But, Mousie, thou art no thy lane,
> In proving foresight may be vain:
> The best laid schemes o' mice an' men
>   Gang aft a-gley
> An' lea'e us nought but grief an' pain
>   For promis'd joy.

Steinbeck finished his short novel—it was only a little more than thirty thousand words—in the summer of 1936. His agents and editor praised the manuscript and accepted it immediately. Published in 1937, *Of Mice and Men* was an instant best-seller.

An important event occurred while Steinbeck was finishing revisions of *Of Mice and Men*: He served a stint as a reporter for the *San Francisco News*. The newspaper asked him to report on the conditions of the migrant laborers who flooded California at harvest time. This task required Steinbeck to visit the migrant camps and record his impressions. To maintain anonymity, Steinbeck wore old, worn clothing. Behind the wheel of a ramshackle bakery truck, Steinbeck observed firsthand the adversity—starvation, violence, disease—the migrants were forced to endure. His chronicles of their sad plight were published in October 1936 as a series of articles titled "The Harvest Gypsies." His moving narrative of families such as this generated great public sympathy:

> Four nights ago the mother had a baby in the tent, on the dirty

carpet. It was born dead, which was just as well because she could not have fed it at the breast; her own diet will not produce milk.

After it was born and she had seen that it was dead, the mother rolled over and lay still for two days. She is up today, tottering around. The last baby, born less than a year ago, lived a week. This woman's eyes have the glazed, faraway look of a sleepwalker's eyes.

She does not wash clothes any more. The drive that makes for cleanliness has been drained out of her and she hasn't the energy. The husband was a share-cropper once, but he couldn't make it go. Now he has lost even his desire to talk. . . .

The children do not even go to the willow clump any more. They squat where they are and kick a little dirt. The father is vaguely aware that there is a culture of hookworm in the mud along the river bank. He knows the children will get it on their bare feet.

But he hasn't the will nor the energy to resist. Too many things have happened to him.

This experience not only stirred Steinbeck's sense of social injustice, but was also a prelude to *The Grapes of Wrath*, Steinbeck's magnum opus.

ON STAGE AND SCREEN

Attracted by *Of Mice and Men*'s rave reviews, playwright-director George S. Kaufman set out to adapt the novel to the stage. Steinbeck produced a script from the novel and the play was scheduled to open at the Music Box Theater in New York in November 1937. Interestingly, even though Steinbeck and his wife were in New York that fall, John—forever dodging the spotlight—elected to return to California, via the Oklahoma dust bowl, before the premiere. Steinbeck's conspicuous absence notwithstanding, the play *Of Mice and Men* was a huge critical and popular success. It won the New York Drama Critics Circle Award for the best American play of the season.

The success of the play prompted a flood of offers from filmmakers who wanted to turn *Of Mice and Men* into a movie. Steinbeck approved a screenplay written by Eugene Solow and worked with director Lewis Milestone in producing the film. It was released on December 22, 1939. Although not a big box-office hit, the film received some good reviews and has come to be recognized as a Hollywood classic. Later film treatments include a 1981 made-for-television movie produced by Robert Blake and a 1992 Metro-Goldwyn-Mayer version.

Back in California, the Steinbecks purchased a home on fifty acres of land. Encouraged by the success of his recent books, Steinbeck took advantage of the quiet refuge to begin his "big book" about migrant laborers. Since his assignment for the *San Francisco News*, Steinbeck had been searching for a vehicle that would bring their plight to prominence. The result was *The Grapes of Wrath*, focusing on the dispossessed dust bowl farmers and their grim pilgrimage to California farm country. The book was published in April 1939. Despite Steinbeck's doubts that the book would be popular, its release was followed by astonishing international acclaim. It quickly rose to the top of the best-seller list. Along with its sensational popularity came a flood of outrage, particularly from the agricultural industry. The ensuing controversy only served to keep the book in the news, drawing even more readers. By the end of the year, more than 430,000 copies had been sold, a figure second only to *Gone with the Wind*. With *The Grapes of Wrath*, Steinbeck had irrevocably cemented his position in the public spotlight.

The demands of public life began to take their toll on Steinbeck and his marriage. Always one to shun publicity, Steinbeck often left Carol to deal with a constant onslaught of letters and visitors and celebrity obligations. Under the strain, their arguments increased in frequency. During a trip to Hollywood to visit the filming of a Steinbeck novel, the two split up. During this time, Steinbeck met and fell in love with Gwendolyn Conger, an aspiring actress-singer. Not totally committed to ending his faltering marriage, however, he managed a reconciliation with Carol, even as tensions between the two remained high.

While trying to mend his marriage during the summer of 1939, Steinbeck spent a great deal of time with Ed Ricketts. Steinbeck wanted to learn as much about marine biology as he could. In 1940 Steinbeck, Carol, and Ricketts embarked on a specimen-collecting expedition to the Gulf of California, called the Sea of Cortez in Mexico. The events of the research trip were published in 1941 under the title *The Log from "The Sea of Cortez."* Steinbeck's marriage, however, had deteriorated irrevocably. The couple were divorced in 1943. During this period, Steinbeck learned that he had won a Pulitzer Prize for *The Grapes of Wrath*.

A BUSY DECADE

Steinbeck spent the forties in a whirlwind of writing, researching, and traveling, including many moves between New York and California. In Mexico City, he observed the filming of his book *The Forgotten Village*, which focuses on life in a small Mexican village. He spent time in Hollywood for the filming of *Tortilla Flat*. As World War II captured the attention of the world, the U.S. government recruited Steinbeck to produce propaganda tales. He wrote *The Moon Is Down*, a grim chronicle of a small European town occupied by Nazis. He also churned out *Bombs Away: The Story of a Bomber Team* and the script for the film *Lifeboat*, a war-morale movie.

In March 1943 Steinbeck married Gwen Conger. In June, Steinbeck left his new bride for a job in England as a war correspondent for the *Herald-Tribune*. Shortly after, he transferred to North Africa to report on military activities there. He often disregarded his own personal safety and entered combat zones so that he could closely observe events as they unfolded. He even reported activity in the midst of battle. His vivid war accounts not only stirred thousands of readers but also left a deep impression on Steinbeck himself.

Returning from his wartime duty, Steinbeck turned his attention to a host of writing projects. In an attempt to take his mind off of the war, he wrote *Cannery Row* in just six weeks. His first son, Thom, was born just after he completed the manuscript in August 1944. *Cannery Row*, the humorous story of a Monterey waterfront community, was published the following January. Following its well-received release, Steinbeck continued work on his next book, *The Pearl*, which relates the story of a poor fisherman who finds a pearl that comes to symbolize good and evil. Both *The Pearl* and *The Wayward Bus*, an amusing story about a busload of memorable characters, were published in 1947. Both books sold well, although *The Wayward Bus* received poor reviews.

PERSONAL STRIFE

The Steinbecks' second son, John, was born in August 1946. While Steinbeck loved his children, his marriage was not a happy one. Conditions went from bad to worse when Steinbeck received the devastating news in 1948 that Ed Ricketts had been killed in a car accident. A grief-stricken Steinbeck wrote in a letter to his friend Bo Beskow, "There died the greatest man I have known and the best teacher. It is going to take a long time to reorganize my thinking and my planning without him." Ricketts's death marked the beginning of a dark time in Steinbeck's life. After Ricketts's funeral, Gwen asked Steinbeck for a divorce. Steinbeck was deeply sorrowed by a second failed marriage and financially stressed by the terms of the divorce settlement. Steinbeck's books were selling well, but not well enough to meet alimony and child support obligations. Steinbeck returned to his family home in Pacific Grove to heal his wounds, seeking solace, as usual, in his writing.

Although the early years of the fifties were difficult, Steinbeck's spirit was returning. His personal life improved when he married Elaine Scott, ex-wife of the actor Zachary Scott, in 1950. This marriage was happy and harmonious, and Steinbeck set about his writing with renewed vigor. He completed a screenplay for *Viva Zapata!*, about the exploits of Mexican revolutionary Emiliano Zapata, and published *Burning Bright*, a short novel in play form that was produced as a Broadway play. In February 1951, Steinbeck began work on *East of Eden*, the saga of two families set in the Salinas Valley. It was published in 1952 and quickly became a bestseller despite harsh critics. Next, he revised *Cannery Row* under the title *Sweet Thursday*, which was published in 1954. Again, reviews were unfavorable. In 1956, Steinbeck began a book based on the retelling of Sir Thomas Malory's *Le Morte Darthur*, the story he had loved as a child. This would be published posthumously as *The Acts of King Arthur and His Noble Knights*. In 1957, *The Short Reign of Pippin IV* was published. It sold extremely well, but like Steinbeck's other recent work, received poor reviews.

Steinbeck was frustrated by the poor critical response to his recent novels. Then, in 1959 he suffered what appeared to be a stroke, forcing him to take time off from his writing to rest. His self-confidence continued to wane. Nevertheless, in a writing frenzy, he took up his pen and wrote *The Winter of Our Discontent*. Even before its publication in June 1961, he set off on a journey across America in a camper with Elaine's poodle Charley. This pilgrimage became the subject of *Travels with Charley in Search of America*. A few months after its publication in 1962, Steinbeck learned that he had been awarded the Nobel Prize for literature.

Steinbeck spent his last years involved in political affairs.

In January 1961, he was an invited guest at John F. Kennedy's inauguration. After the president's assassination in 1963, Steinbeck became friends with Kennedy's successor, Lyndon B. Johnson. In the midsixties he reported on the war on Vietnam for *Newsday*, a Long Island daily. Seized by severe back pain on his return from traveling, he never fully recovered and suffered for his last year and a half. Steinbeck died in New York on December 20, 1968, at the age of sixty-six. Shortly before his death, he told Elaine, "No man should be buried in alien soil," to which she replied, "I know what you are telling me. You won't be." True to her word, Elaine returned Steinbeck's ashes to his native ground in Salinas, California, where they rest today.

CHAPTER 1

Themes in *Of Mice and Men*

READINGS ON
OF MICE AND MEN

The Need for Commitment

Louis Owens

George and Lennie dream of a little farm where they can "live off the fatta the lan'." This vision of Eden has long been recognized as an important theme in *Of Mice and Men*. Louis Owens differs from some critics, however, in his assessment that man's isolation and the dream of commitment—the yearning all men have for contact with another living being—are the predominant themes of the novel. Owens maintains that the dream of the farm is symbolic of the deep, mutual commitment of George and Lennie. Although the dream of the farm dies, Owens adds, George and Lennie do attain, for a short while, the dream of commitment when they break the grip of loneliness that characterizes the world of the ranch and bunkhouse. Louis Owens is the author of *John Steinbeck's Re-Vision of America*, from which this critical analysis is excerpted.

The Eden myth looms large in *Of Mice and Men* (1937), the play-novella set along the Salinas River "a few miles south of Soledad." And, as in all of Steinbeck's California fiction, setting plays a central role in determining the major themes of this work. The fact that the setting for *Of Mice and Men* is a California valley dictates, according to the symbolism of Steinbeck's landscapes, that this story will take place in a fallen world and that the quest for the illusive and illusory American Eden will be of central thematic significance. In no other work does Steinbeck demonstrate greater skill in merging the real setting of his native country with the thematic structure of his novel.

Critics have consistently recognized in Lennie's dream of living "off the fatta the lan'" on a little farm the American

Reprinted by permission of the author from *John Steinbeck's Re-Vision of America* by Louis Owens (Athens: University of Georgia Press, 1985).

dream of a new Eden. Joseph Fontenrose states concisely, "The central image is the earthly paradise. . . . It is a vision of Eden." Peter Lisca takes this perception further, noting that "the world of *Of Mice and Men* is a fallen one, inhabited by sons of Cain, forever exiled from Eden, the little farm of which they dream." There are no Edens in Steinbeck's writing, only illusions of Eden, and in the fallen world of the Salinas Valley—which Steinbeck would later place "east of Eden"—the Promised Land is an illusory and painful dream. In this land populated by "sons of Cain," men condemned to wander in solitude, the predominant theme is that of loneliness, or what Donald Pizer has called "fear of apartness." Pizer has, in fact, discovered *the* major theme of this novel when he says, "One of the themes of *Of Mice and Men* is that men fear loneliness, that they need someone to be with and to talk to who will offer understanding and companionship."

The setting Steinbeck chose for this story brilliantly underscores the theme of man's isolation and need for commitment. Soledad is a very real, dusty little town on the western edge of the Salinas River midway down the Salinas Valley. Like most of the settings in Steinbeck's fiction, this place exists; it *is.* However, with his acute sensitivity to place names and his knowledge of Spanish, Steinbeck was undoubtedly aware that "Soledad" translates into English as "solitude" or "loneliness." In this country of solitude and loneliness, George and Lennie stand out sharply because they have each other or, as George says, "We got somebody to talk to that gives a damn about us." Cain's question is the question again at the heart of this novel: "Am I my brother's keeper?" And the answer found in the relationship between George and Lennie is an unmistakable confirmation.

Of Mice and Men is most often read as one of Steinbeck's most pessimistic works, smacking of pessimistic determinism. Fontenrose suggests that the novel is about "the vanity of human wishes" and asserts that, more pessimistically than Burns, "Steinbeck reads, '*All* schemes o' mice and men gang *ever* agley'" [my italics]. Howard Levant, in a very critical reading of the novel, concurs, declaring that "the central theme is stated and restated—the good life is impossible because humanity is flawed." In spite of the general critical reaction, and without disputing the contention that Steinbeck allows no serious hope that George and Lennie will ever achieve their dream farm, it is nonetheless possible to read

Of Mice and Men in a more optimistic light than has been customary. In previous works we have seen a pattern established in which the Steinbeck hero achieves greatness in the midst of, even because of, apparent defeat. In *Of Mice and Men,* Steinbeck accepts, very non-teleologically, the fact that man is flawed and the Eden myth mere illusion. However, critics have consistently under-valued Steinbeck's emphasis on the theme of commitment, which runs through the novel and which is the chief ingredient in the creation of the Steinbeck hero.

THEIR BROTHER'S KEEPER

The dream of George and Lennie represents a desire to defy the curse of Cain and fallen man—to break the pattern of wandering and loneliness imposed on the outcasts and to return to the perfect garden. George and Lennie achieve all of this dream that is possible in the real world: they are their brother's keeper. Unlike the solitary Cain and the solitary men who inhabit the novel, they have someone who cares. The dream of the farm merely symbolizes their deep mutual commitment, a commitment that is immediately sensed by the other characters in the novel. The ranch owner is suspicious of the relationship, protesting, "I never seen one guy take so much trouble for another guy." Slim, the godlike jerkline skinner, admires the relationship and says, "Ain't many guys travel around together. . . . I don't know why. Maybe everybody in the whole damn world is scared of each other." Candy, the one-handed swamper, and Crooks, the deformed black stablehand, also sense the unique commitment between the two laborers, and in their moment of unity Candy and Crooks turn as one to defend Lennie from the threat posed by Curley's wife. The influence of George and Lennie's mutual commitment, and of their dream, has for an instant made these crippled sons of Cain their brother's keepers and broken the grip of loneliness and solitude in which they exist. Lennie's yearning for the rabbits and for all soft, living things symbolizes the yearning all men have for warm, living contact. It is this yearning, described by Steinbeck as "the inarticulate and powerful yearning of all men," which makes George need Lennie just as much as Lennie needs George and which sends Curley's wife wandering despairingly about the ranch in search of companionship. Whereas Fontenrose has suggested that "the individualistic desire for carefree enjoyment of pleasures is the serpent in the garden" in this book, the real serpent is loneliness and the barriers between men and between men and women that create and reinforce this loneliness.

Lennie has been seen as representing "the frail nature of primeval innocence" and as the id to George's ego or the body to George's brain. In the novel, Lennie is repeatedly associated with animals or described as childlike. He appears in the opening scene dragging his feet "the way a bear drags his paws," and in the final scene he enters the clearing in the brush "as silently as a creeping bear." Slim says of Lennie, "He's jes' like a kid, ain't he," and George repeats, "Sure, he's jes' like a kid." The unavoidable truth is, however, that Lennie, be he innocent "natural," uncontrollable id, or simply a huge child, is above all dangerous. Unlike Benjy in *The Sound and the Fury* (whom Steinbeck may have had in mind when describing the incident in Weed in which Lennie clings bewildered to the girl's dress), Lennie is monstrously powerful and has a propensity for killing things. Even if Lennie had not killed Curley's wife, he would sooner or later have done something fatal to bring violence upon himself, as the lynch mob that hunted him in Weed suggests.

Steinbeck's original title for *Of Mice and Men* was "Something That Happened," a title suggesting that Steinbeck was taking a purely non-teleological or nonblaming point of view in this novel. If we look at the novel in this way, it becomes clear that Lennie dies because he has been created incapable of dealing with society and is, in fact, a menace to society. Like Pepé in "Flight," Tularecito in *The Pastures of Heaven*, and Frankie in *Cannery Row*, Lennie is a "natural" who loses when he is forced to confront society. This is simply the way it is—something that happened—and when George kills Lennie he is not only saving him from the savagery of the pursuers, he is, as John Ditsky says, acknowledging that "Lennie's situation is quite hopeless." Ditsky further suggests that Lennie's death represents "a matter of cold hard necessity imposing itself upon the frail hopes of man." Along these same lines, Joan Steele declares that "Lennie has to be destroyed because he is a 'loner' whose weakness precludes his cooperating with George and hence working constructively toward their mutual goal." Lennie, however, is not a "loner"; it is, in fact, the opposite, overwhelming and uncontrollable urge for contact that brings about Lennie's destruction and the destruction of living creatures he comes into contact with. Nonetheless, Steele makes an important point when she suggests that because of Lennie the dream of the Edenic farm was never a possibility. Lennie's flaw represents the inherent imperfection in humanity that renders Eden forever an impossibility. Lennie would have brought his imperfection with him to the little farm, and he would have killed the rabbits.

DREAM OF COMMITMENT REALIZED

When Lennie dies, the teleological dream of the Edenic farm dies with him, for while Lennie's weakness doomed the dream it was only his innocence that kept it alive. The death of the dream, however, does not force *Of Mice and Men* to end on the strong note of pessimism critics have consistently claimed. For while the dream of the farm perishes, the theme of commitment achieves its strongest statement in the book's conclusion. Unlike Candy, who abandons responsibility for his old dog and allows Carlson to shoot him, George remains his brother's keeper without faltering even to the point of killing Lennie while Lennie sees visions of Eden. In accepting complete responsibility for Lennie, George demonstrates the degree of commitment necessary to the Steinbeck hero, and in fact enters the ranks of those heroes. It is ironic that, in this fallen world, George must reenact the crime of Cain to demonstrate the depth of his commitment. It is a frank acceptance of the way things are.

Slim recognizes the meaning of George's act. When the pursuers discover George just after he has shot Lennie, Steinbeck writes: "Slim came directly to George and sat down beside him, sat very close to him." Steinbeck's forceful prose here, with the key word "directly," and the emphatic repetition in the last phrase place heavy emphasis on Slim's gesture. Steinbeck is stressing the significance of the new relationship between George and Slim. As the novel ends, George is going off with Slim to have a drink, an action Fontenrose mistakenly interprets as evidence "that George had turned to his counterdream of independence: freedom from Lennie." French suggests that "Slim's final attempt to console George ends the novel on the same compassionate note as that of *The Red Pony*, but Slim can only alleviate, not cure, the situation." Steinbeck, however, seems to be deliberately placing much greater emphasis on the developing friendship between the two men than such interpretations would allow for. Lisca has pointed out the circular structure of the novel—the neat balancing of the opening and closing scenes. Bearing this circularity in mind, it should be noted that this novel about man's loneliness and "apartness" began with two men—George and Lennie—climbing down to the pool from the highway and that the novel ends with two men—George and Slim—climbing back up from the pool to the highway. Had George been left alone and apart from the rest of humanity at the end of the novel, had he suffered the fate of Cain, this would indeed have been the most pessimistic of Steinbeck's works. That George is not alone has tremendous significance. In the fallen world of the valley, where human commitment is the only realizable dream, the fact that in the end as in the beginning two men walk together causes *Of Mice and Men* to end on a strong note of hope—the crucial dream, the dream of man's commitment to man, has not perished with Lennie. The dream will appear again, in fact, in much greater dimension in Steinbeck's next novel, *The Grapes of Wrath.*

The Dream of Independence

Joseph Fontenrose

John Steinbeck once wrote in a letter that *Of Mice and Men* was "a study of the dreams and pleasures of everyone in the world." Steinbeck's portrayal of the yearnings of common people is clearly evident in *Of Mice and Men;* George, Lennie, and other farm-workers share a dreamlike ideal of land and a little farm to work. According to Joseph Fontenrose, this dream of independence and prosperity contrasts sharply, however, with the dream of a carefree lifestyle and freedom from inconvenient burdens. These two dreams oppose each other; the pursuit of pleasures—cards, whiskey, and women—can thwart the best-laid plans to acquire land and settle down. Fontenrose taught classics at the University of California at Berkeley, Cornell University, and the University of Oregon. He is the author of *John Steinbeck: An Introduction and Interpretation.*

When *Of Mice and Men* appeared in February, 1937, one year after *In Dubious Battle,* readers were not surprised to find that it dealt with agricultural labor in California; for the earlier novel had established Steinbeck as a writer interested in contemporary issues. Yet, if upon opening the new novel the reader expected more about strikes and Communist agitators, he was disappointed; for the workers in *Of Mice and Men* have not yet reached social awareness or class consciousness: they accept their lot, spend their small earnings, never question the structure of society. Here is no Growers' Association to exploit migratory pickers; the men work on a large grain-producing farm (always called "ranch"), managed solely by its owner, who hires hands at fifty dollars a month and found. That is, he has workers who stay with him the year round; others prefer to work for a season and then move on; these are migratory of their own choice. The Great Depression is not yet. . . .

Man's longing for the land, a favorite Steinbeck theme, appearing in some form in nearly every novel, is here expressed in the farmhand's and bindlestiff's desire for a few acres of his own, so that he can be his own boss. George said, "I'd have my own little place, an' I'd be bringin' in my own crops, 'stead of doin' all the work and not getting what comes up outa the ground." And Candy said,

> Everybody wants a little bit of land, not much. Jus' som'thin' that was his. Som'thin' he could live on and there couldn't nobody throw him off of it. I never had none. I planted crops for damn near ever'body in this state, but they wasn't my crops, and when I harvested 'em, it wasn't none of my harvest.

Only in such speeches as these does *Of Mice and Men* seem to relate this land hunger to contemporary social issues. But this is hardly the author's intention: he is simply reporting a mode in which the yearning is really expressed by men whose chances of acquiring land are well-nigh hopeless— altogether hopeless, as Crooks, the Negro stable buck, saw it:

> I seen hunderds of men come by on the road an' on the ranches, with their bindles on their back an' that same damn thing in their heads. Hunderds of them. They come, an' they quit an' go on; an' every damn one of 'em's got a little piece of land in his head. An' never a God damn one of 'em ever gets it. Just like heaven. . . . Nobody never gets to heaven, and nobody gets no land. It's just in their head.

Yet Crooks too had the dream. When he saw that Candy and Lennie had a real proposition, backed by real money, he offered to work for them for nothing, just to share their independence—until Curley's wife made him realize the futility of his wish. And Crooks was right after all, as the story is told: these were but three more men with that "thing in their heads." The land hunger of impoverished farm workers, a dream of independence, usually remains a dream; and when it becomes a real plan, the plan is defeated.

A PARABLE OF THE HUMAN CONDITION

Of Mice and Men was meant to be a non-teleological tale, and the first title that Steinbeck gave it was "Something That Happened." Something that happens may be accidental, coincidental, atypical, and surely the concluding events and deeds in this novel are neither typical nor commonplace. For George and Lennie, being who they are and where they are, the outcome may be inevitable, and we may see a personal tragedy in the tale. Steinbeck, however, meant the story to be a parable of the human condition, as his final title indicates. It is a good title, because the story itself tells us just what Burns meant when he said, "the best-laid schemes o' mice an' men gang aft agley": one unlucky fieldmouse lost its nest when the field was plowed. But not all fieldmice suffer that fate; Burns did not mean that no man's scheme is ever realized. Steinbeck reads, "All schemes o' mice an' men gang ever agley." Crooks said, "Nobody never gets to heaven, and nobody gets no land," and George said to Candy, "—I think I knowed from the very first. I think I knowed we'd never do her," thus reading destiny—the inevitable failure of his plans—in Lennie's terrible deed. It is the message of *Cup of Gold*, the vanity of human wishes. In a letter to his agents, written soon after completing the manuscript of *Of Mice and Men*, Steinbeck said that Lennie represents "the inarticulate and powerful yearning of all men," and referred to its scene as a microcosm, making it plain that this novel was meant to express the inevitable defeat and futility of all men's plans. But the tragic story of George and Lennie cannot carry the load of cosmic pessimism placed upon it. It tells us only that it is hard for bindlestiffs to buy land, and that even when they get the money they cannot be sure of making the purchase. Nevertheless, migratory workers have acquired land, even in California, and George could have done so. Not Lennie who died, but Candy who lived, had $350, and Candy still wanted to carry out the plan. Objectively considered, the prospects for success were better without Lennie, who would surely have killed every rabbit on the place. But without Lennie the plan had no meaning for George. The sweeping pessimistic thesis is thus imposed upon the story and obscures its true meaning: that our pleasures often oppose and thwart our schemes. Steinbeck came nearer to an adequate statement of thesis when he said in another letter that *Of Mice and Men* was "a study of the dreams and pleasures of everyone in the world."

After shooting Lennie, an act that the others assumed he had done in self-defense, George went off with Slim to get a drink. This means that George had turned to his counter-dream of independence: freedom from Lennie. This dream, as well as the other, George recited in both the opening and closing scenes among the willows by the river:

> God a'mighty, if I was alone I could live so easy. I could go get a job an' work, an' no trouble. No mess at all, and when the end of the month come I could take my fifty bucks and go into town and get whatever I want. Why, I could stay in a cat house all night. I could eat any place I want, hotel or any place, and order any damn thing I could think of. An' I could do all that every damn month. Get a gallon of whisky, or set in a pool room and play cards or shoot pool.... An' whatta I got,... I got you! You can't keep a job and you lose me ever' job I get.

It is a recital that Lennie often heard. At the end the contrite Lennie expected to hear it again and urged George to say it. George started half-heartedly, but soon turned to the other recital about the land and the rabbits. And what George longed for in his dream of individual freedom was exactly what he deprecated in his dream of living with Lennie on a small ranch. He recited this dream too at the beginning and end of the story, and once in the middle; but only the first time is it given in its complete ritualistic form:

> Guys like us, that work on ranches, are the loneliest guys in the world. They got no fambly. They don't belong no place. They come to a ranch an' work up a stake and then they go into town and blow their stake, and the first thing you know they're poundin' their tail on some other ranch. They ain't got nothing to look ahead to.... With us it ain't like that. We got a future. We got somebody to talk to that gives a damn about us. We don't have to sit in no bar room blowin' in our jack jus' because we got no place else to go.

Then he went on to describe the little place that they would buy when they "[got] the jack together," where they would "*live off the fatta the lan'.*"

A Choice Between Dreams

So the "dreams and pleasures" of Steinbeck's statement are both synonymous and contrasting terms. The lonely bindle-stiff dreams of owning land (and although George said that others did not have "a future," Crooks said that all ranch workers had that dream); yet he enjoys cards, whisky, women. His pleasures take his little money and he never begins to realize the dream. For George, who was tied to Lennie, freedom to enjoy these pleasures was as much a dream as having a ranch; in fact, any indulgence in them was severely limited, since Lennie prevented his earning more than a few dollars at a time. Thus George was split between genuine affection for Lennie, who was company, someone to control and look after, and a desire to be free of an inconvenient burden. When he shot Lennie he was not only saving Lennie from Curley's cruelty, but was also making a choice between dreams: events had forced him to a decision. "I'll work my month an' I'll take my fifty bucks an' I'll stay all night in some lousy cat house. Or I'll set in some poolroom...,"—thus George answered Candy's question "Then—it's all off?" and realized without joy that one dream was dead and another, the dream of lonely independence, had come true.

Of Mice and Men has no recognizable mythical pattern. The central image is the earthly paradise, visible in nearly every Steinbeck novel. This has meant for Americans an agrarian economy of small farms, worked by their owners for their own benefit. It is part of the American dream, finding expression in such nineteenth-century visions as "the garden of the west" and "the garden of the world." It is a vision of Eden, a land of peace, harmony, prosperity; it includes both individual independence and fellowship. And in Steinbeck's world you aren't likely to get there; as Crooks said, "Nobody never gets to heaven."

We should also notice that this novel ignores the group organism, unless we say that Lennie, representing "the inarticulate and powerful yearning of all men," symbolizes it. Like the group Lennie has an elementary mentality, lacks initiative and originality, and can follow but not lead. The association of George and Lennie, leader and follower, is held together by a religion, complete with myth, ritual, and litany. When George makes his formulaic recitation, as quoted above, Lennie responds at the right place with *"But not us! An' why? Because... because I got you to look after me, and you got me to look after you, and that's why."* From loneliness, from blowing our money in barrooms and cat houses, from jails, good Lord deliver us—and grant us the blessings of fellowship on the land. It is a religion of cooperation, but, as in other religions, deprecated evils are powerful to keep men from paradise. The individual's desire for carefree enjoyment of pleasures is the serpent in the garden.

Control and Freedom

Samuel I. Bellman

Samuel I. Bellman argues that George's relationships to Lennie and Slim suggest an interesting paradox regarding freedom and control: real independence requires not only desires and impulses, but the controls to keep them in check. Bellman concludes that at no point in the story does George by himself truly experience adult freedom. Rather, he remains under the control of an outside regulatory force: first Lennie, whose primitive instincts exercise an inhibiting effect on George, and later Slim, the jerkline skinner endowed by Steinbeck with godlike qualities. Bellman contributed this essay to a 1975 issue of *CEA Critic*, a journal of the College English Association.

The sensitive reader re-reading John Steinbeck's deceptively simple adventure story just bordering on the social protest novel, *Of Mice and Men* (1937), may be forced to alter his assumptions about Steinbeck's view of the orderliness of life and the 'fitness' of things. Here I do not wish to open the bothersome issue of Steinbeck's "non-teleological thinking," discussed in chapter fourteen of *The Log from The Sea of Cortez* (1951): getting at the *what* or the *how* of the situation, instead of the *why*. Steinbeck is more accessible to the general reader when he leaves such mind-bending matters as epistemology and ontology to the philosophers and 'tells it like it is' or at least 'like he sees it.'

'Like he sees it' is often taken to mean (thanks to Edmund Wilson's pioneering essay in his 1941 collection, *The Boys in the Back Room*) a reduction of human and societal endeavor to animal-survival terms. But there is something deeper at work in Steinbeck's fiction: the suggestion of a closed energy system; and an automatic regulation of that energy. Gain

From Samuel I. Bellman, "Control and Freedom in Steinbeck's *Of Mice and Men*," *CEA Critic*, vol. 38, no. 1, November 1975. Reprinted by permission of the College English Association.

something here, lose something there (consider Hemingway's World Series analogy, which went something like this: win in Chicago, lose in Detroit), balancing the books before the final curtain drops. Compare what happens in *The Pearl*, at the end of *The Grapes of Wrath*, and at the end of *Burning Bright:* tragic loss (or a sense of tragic loss) followed by a qualified compensation.

Yet Steinbeck's fiction also conveys the idea that something more than energy balance (energy being neither created nor destroyed) is involved. In other words, the amount of available energy—i.e., available opportunity for joy, productive action, self-fulfillment in a deep sense—is steadily diminishing. Thermodynamic *entropy.* Social systems or groups break down, even "nations of two" (in Kurt Vonnegut's wonderful phrase) . . . the light of original happiness or of trusting hope eventually dims.

LENNIE AS *ID*-FIGURE

Applying this notion of Steinbeck's pessimistic energy-system scheme (things are running down, but *loss* will bring a kind of *replacement)* to *Of Mice and Men* reveals an interesting paradox having to do with freedom and control. First we will have to recap the story briefly, accenting certain psychological features. The scene is a ranch near Soledad, California, and the two chief characters are a pair of itinerant farm workers, George (the responsible one, who makes the decisions and lays the plans) and Lennie (the retarded and irresponsible one, whom George will always have to take care of). In a sense, George and Lennie are to each other as *ego* is to *id* in the same mind: the conscious, reality-sensitive regulator always having to keep in check the primitive, violent instincts.

The crux of this story about the best laid plans of mice and men often going awry is the dilemma George faces after Lennie accidentally kills the boss's daughter-in-law. The aroused ranch hands, led by Curley (the dead woman's husband) run out to find Lennie and shoot him. George, who has stolen a gun from one of the men, gets to Lennie first. The two have a heart-to-heart talk, reiterating (each on his own level) their hopes and problems. It is as though a human mind were having a dialogue with itself, matching one viewpoint with another or, let us say, *ego* with *id.* George feels he will have to kill Lennie to spare his being

GALAHAD DISMOUNTED

Warren French describes Of Mice and Men *as a novel influenced by Arthurian legend. In this excerpt from his book* John Steinbeck, *French analyzes George, who, like the knights of Camelot, is loyal and pure.*

Although other critics have not noted to what extent *Of Mice and Men* is an Arthurian story, the fundamental parallels—the knightly loyalty, the pursuit of the vision, the creation of a bond (shared briefly by Candy and Crooks), and its destruction by an at least potentially adulterous relationship—are there. They are, however, so concealed by the surface realism of the work that one unfamiliar with Steinbeck's previous Arthurian experiments would be hardly likely to notice them. The one obvious Arthurian hangover is George, who is not only remarkably loyal to his charge—the feeble-minded Lennie—but also remarkably pure.

George not only warns Lennie against the blandishments of Curley's wife, but is himself obviously impervious to her charms. While the other ranch hands are excited by her presence, George says only, "Jesus, what a tramp!" When invited to join the boys in a Saturday night trip to a neighboring town's "nice" whorehouse, George says that he "might go in an' set and have a shot," but "ain't puttin' out no two and a half." He excuses himself on the ground that he is saving money to buy a farm, but not even Galahad might have found it politic to profess chastity in a bunkhouse. George seems to have stepped, in fact, not out of [British writer Sir Thomas] Malory's Arthurian stories but [British writer Alfred Lord] Tennyson's. When he is told that Curley boasts of having his glove full of Vaseline in order to keep his hand soft for his wife, George says, "That's a dirty thing to tell around."

George is noticeably more critical of Curley's wife than Steinbeck is. *Of Mice and Men* is not so completely objective as *In Dubious Battle;* Steinbeck editorializes occasionally, for example, after the girl has been killed:

> . . . the meanness and the plannings and the discontent and the ache for attention were all gone from her face. She was very pretty and simple, and her face was sweet and young.

George shows no such sympathy, and it is important to notice that the author is more flexible than his character, because it is a sign that he is not being carried away by his vision as are the characters sometimes assumed to represent his viewpoint. The Arthurian flavor here is faint, but unmistakable. Like Jim Nolan [in *In Dubious Battle*], George is a last Galahad, dismounted, armed only with a fading dream, a long way from Camelot. Steinbeck is his historian, not his alter ego.

killed (and, we suspect, being worked over, first) by the others. But it is hard for George to pull the trigger and yet even harder for him not to, which would mean exposing Lennie to a brutal murder by the gang. Finally, after a real heart-to-heart talk, George manages to shoot the unsuspecting, eternally repentant and hopeful Lennie.

So suspenseful and yet painful is the conclusion to the tale that the reader may easily miss a number of peculiar implications. First, George was a "whole" person only so long as he was tied up to Lennie, looking out for him, denying himself all the pleasures of the senses so he could save his money and they could buy a place of their own. It was the unusual buddyship of the two, the story makes clear, that rendered possible a glorious dream of self-improvement, a constructive hope to live by. But their dream of a place of their own was shattered after Lennie killed the woman. The kind of self-improvement held up as an ideal in the story was possible neither through the buddyship of George and Lennie nor through George's going it alone.

Second, George came to feel that he had to kill Lennie for Lennie's own good. And with Lennie dead, George could raise all the hell he had wanted to before but had been prevented (ostensibly by Lennie) from doing. Third, Lennie, as an *id*-figure, had actually exercised a restraining, inhibiting effect on George: the effect of the *super-ego*, the restrictions of society. But with Lennie dead, George was apparently about to become an *id*-figure himself, giving free rein to his "lower" desires and impulses. However, there is one more implication that cannot be overlooked: the matter of Authority.

SLIM AS AUTHORITY FIGURE

After he discovered the dead woman George was unable to make up his mind as to what to do with Lennie. What really persuaded George to kill Lennie—it is as though he required official sanction for the unlawful act—is a real Authority figure, a man with "calm, Godlike eyes." This is Slim, "a jerkline skinner, the prince of the ranch . . .". Slim "moved with a majesty only achieved by royalty and master craftsmen. . . . There was a gravity in his manner and a quiet so profound that all talk stopped when he spoke. His authority was so great that his word was taken on any subject, be it politics or love. . . . His ear heard more than was said to him, and his slow speech had overtones not of thought, but of understanding beyond thought."

Not only did Slim talk George into killing Lennie, but he reassured him afterward that he had had to do it. And then he led George away so that they could go and have a drink somewhere. As if to clarify his subtle point about George now being linked closely to *another* regulatory force—the mysteriously powerful Slim instead of the simplemindedly powerful Lennie—Steinbeck has one of the men, at the close of the novel, inquire naively: "Now what the hell ya suppose is eatin' them two guys?"

So, in a sense, George is still dependent on some superior force, still "innocent" (in his fashion) of the experience of adult freedom, still an *id*-figure (ironically enough, considering Lennie's *id* qualities) to be kept under control (by Slim this time). The point Steinbeck seems to be making, as he rings down the curtain, is this. The individual may get rid of part of the *self*, for whatever reason, in whatever way (rejecting it, talking it out, shooting it out, etc.). But something else—a prosthetic device, so to speak—will be put right back in to take its place. And things will never be as good as they were before. What appears to be a newly gained freedom not only brings sadness, it brings return of control as well.

A Study of Social Conflict

B. Ramachandra Rao

B. Ramachandra Rao of Punjabi University in India analyzes the work of Steinbeck and other twentieth-century authors in his book *The American Fictional Hero*. He identifies three social groups who populate all of Steinbeck's novels. *Of Mice and Men*'s ignorant and exploited workers belong to the category of underdogs: weak and defeated individuals who stand no chance of overcoming the demands of society. Their struggle to participate in the social conflicts of the outside world lends dimension and dignity to the characters, who are able to sustain their faith in a dream against overwhelming odds.

From the complex social pattern in Steinbeck's work, three groups stand out, each differentiated from the others by its responses to the demands of society. The first group consists of the paisanos, the social irresponsibles, who intentionally withdraw from active participation in society. The second group consists of the heroes of Steinbeck who stand uneasily at the centre of society, unhappily involved in the social conflict and fighting hard to retain their precious individuality. The third group consists of those who protest in vain, fight feebly, and are defeated by society. To this third group belong the ignorant farmers and the exploited workers. Unlike the paisanos, these people have many things at stake, and hence they are inevitably involved in the social conflict. *Of Mice and Men* (1937) dramatises the intrusions of society in the lives of these weak and defeated individuals. George and Lennie are ranch-hands with dreams of their own. Without families and property, they are drawn towards each other by their common hunger for the land. Lennie is a giant with the mind of a child—a familiar American archetype. The friend-

Excerpted from *The American Fictional Hero* by B. Ramachandra Rao (New Delhi: Bahri Publications, 1979). Reprinted by permission of the publishers.

ship of Lennie and George reminds one of the friendship between the more famous pair, Huck Finn and Jim. This is the typical American theme of strange friendships: and through it are enacted the attempts to put up a joint defence against society in *Of Mice and Men*, paralleling the defensive mechanisms of an evolving consciousness against "civilisation" in *The Adventures of Huckleberry Finn*. The idyllic life of Huck and Jim is interrupted by the intrusion of the outside world, and the happy dreams of Lennie and George are similarly shattered by society. Lennie is an idiot with a fondness for fondling nice things—nice puppies, and the soft hair of pretty women. The author projects him as a symbol of the vague yearnings of all men. Steinbeck once wrote:

> The microcosm is rather difficult to handle and apparently I did not get it over—the earth longings of a Lennie who was not to represent insanity at all but the inarticulate and powerful yearnings of all men.

Lonely and friendless, George and Lennie need, and seek, each other's company. Without a family and without property, they are wanderers in America belonging to no place. They frequently dream of an idyllic ten acres of land and a ranch of their own. This day-dreaming becomes a kind of ritual enactment of self-assurance, as if mere repetition would make the illusion a reality. Lennie's childish belief in this illusion is necessary for George to sustain his own faith in the dream. The stablebuck and old Candy are also drawn to Lennie and George by the strong fascination that the dream exercises upon them. Lennie depends upon George to help him out of difficulties. George, however, needs Lennie as much as the other needs him. Lennie's innocence is not a weakness: it possesses a mysterious strength of its own. It makes life tolerable and even pleasant. So long as Lennie has an almost religious faith in the dream, it continues to be a vital reality. The strength of the dream flows from Lennie's innocence. His death makes George realise that the illusion had acquired the compelling power of reality on account of Lennie's belief in it. An idiot, an ordinary worker, and two old men form a pitifully weak group to defend themselves against society. Reality breaks in [in] the form of Curley's wife. And Lennie's passion for petting leads to the strangling of Curley's wife, and in order to save him from being lynched George shoots Lennie dead. With Lennie's death, the dream vanishes. George says, [before] the shooting down of Lennie:

> I knowed from the very first. I think I knowed we would never
> do her. He usta like to hear about it so much I got to thinking
> maybe we would.

Society proves too strong. The society is represented by
the ranch-owner's son, Curley, whose arrogance is supported by the social system which gives no chance at all for
the underdog. It is this society with its complex structure
which gives a new dimension to the struggles of the Steinbeck hero.

A Parable of
the Curse of Cain

William Goldhurst

William Goldhurst is an emeritus professor of humanities at the University of Florida. He calls *Of Mice and Men* a parable that illustrates the biblical conflict between the brothers Cain and Abel. In the Old Testament story, Cain murders his brother Abel and is exiled by God to a life of wandering. Goldhurst describes the migratory ranch worker, marked by homelessness and economic futility, as the modern counterpart of Cain. In reenacting the drama of Cain through the relationship between George and Lennie, Steinbeck explores whether man is destined to live alone or in fraternity with others. Goldhurst concludes that Steinbeck, in essence, asks the same question that Cain poses to God: Am I my brother's keeper?

Viewed in the light of its mythic and allegorical implications, *Of Mice and Men* is a story about the nature of man's fate in a fallen world, with particular emphasis upon the question: is man destined to live alone, a solitary wanderer on the face of the earth, or is it the fate of man to care for man, to go his way in companionship with another? This is the same theme that occurs in the Old Testament, as early as Chapter Four of Genesis, immediately following the Creation and Expulsion. In effect, the question Steinbeck poses is the same question Cain poses to the Lord: "Am I my brother's keeper?" From its position in the Scriptural version of human history we may assume with the compilers of the early books of the Bible that it is the primary *question concerning man as he is,* after he has lost the innocence and non-being of Eden. It is the same question that Steinbeck chose as the theme of his

Excerpted from William Goldhurst, "*Of Mice and Men*: John Steinbeck's Parable of the Curse of Cain," *Western American Literature*, vol. 6, no. 2, Summer 1971. Reprinted by permission of *Western American Literature*.

later book *East of Eden* (1952), in which novel the Cain and Abel story is reenacted in a contemporary setting and where, for emphasis, Steinbeck has his main characters read the Biblical story aloud and comment upon it, climaxing the discussion with the statement made by Lee: "I think this is the best-known story in the world because it is everybody's story. I think it is the symbol story of the human soul." *Of Mice and Men* is an early Steinbeck variation on this symbol story of the human soul. The implications of the Cain-and-Abel drama are everywhere apparent in the fable of George and Lennie and provide its mythic vehicle.

THE DRAMA OF CAIN

Contrary to Lee's confident assertion, however, most people know the Cain and Abel story only in general outline. The details of the drama need to be filled in, particularly for the purpose of seeing how they apply to Steinbeck's novella. Cain was a farmer, Adam and Eve's first-born son. His offerings of agricultural produce to the Lord failed to find favor, whereas the livestock offered by Cain's brother, Abel, was well received. Angry, jealous, and rejected Cain killed Abel when they were working in the field, and when the Lord inquired of Cain, where is your brother, Cain replied: "I know not: Am I my brother's keeper?" For his crime of homicide the Lord banished Cain from His company and from the company of his parents and set upon him a particular curse, the essence of which was that Cain was to become homeless, a wanderer, and an agricultural worker who would never possess or enjoy the fruits of his labor. Cain was afraid that other men would hear of his crime and try to kill him, but the Lord marked him in a certain way so as to preserve him from the wrath of others. Thus Cain left home and went to the land of Nod, which the story tells us lies east of Eden.

The drama of Cain finds its most relevant application in *Of Mice and Men* in the relationship between Lennie and George, and in the other characters' reactions to their associations. In the first of his six scenes Steinbeck establishes the two ideas that will be developed throughout. The first of these is the affectionate symbiosis of the two protagonists, their brotherly mutual concern and faithful companionship. Steinbeck stresses the beauty, joy, security, and comfort these two derive from the relationship:

"If them other guys gets in jail they can rot for all anybody gives a damn. But not us."

Lennie broke in, "But not us! An' why? Because...because I got you to look after me and you got me to look after you, and that's why." He laughed delightedly.

The second idea, which is given equal emphasis, is the fact that this sort of camaraderie is rare, different, almost unique in the world George and Lennie inhabit; other men, in contrast to these two, are solitary souls without friends or companions. Says George in Scene One:

> Guys like us, that work on ranches, are the loneliest guys in the world. They got no family. They don't belong no place. They come to a ranch an' work up a stake and then they go into town and blow their stakes, and the first thing you know they're poundin' their tail on some other ranch.

The alternative to the George-Lennie companionship is Aloneness, made more dreadful by the addition of an economic futility that Steinbeck augments and reinforces in later sections. The migratory ranch worker, in other words, is the fulfillment of the Lord's curse on Cain: "When thou tillest the ground, it shall not henceforth yield unto thee her strength; a fugitive and vagabond shalt thou be in the earth." Steinbeck's treatment of the theme is entirely free from a sense of contrivance; all the details in *Of Mice and Men* seem natural in the context and organically related to the whole; but note that in addition to presenting Lennie and George as men who till the ground and derive no benefits from their labor, he also manages to have them "on the run" when they are introduced in the first scene—this no doubt to have his main characters correspond as closely as possible to the Biblical passage: "a fugitive and a vagabond shalt thou be. . . ."

To the calamity of homelessness and economic futility Steinbeck later adds the psychological soul-corruption that is the consequence of solitary existence. In Scene Three George tells Slim, the mule-driver on the ranch:

> "I seen the guys that go around on the ranches alone. That ain't no good. They don't have no fun. After a long time they get mean."
> "Yeah, they get mean," Slim agreed. "They get so they don't want to talk to nobody."

Again, in Scene Four, the Negro stable buck Crooks tells Lennie:

> A guy needs somebody—to be near him. . . . A guy goes nuts if he ain't got nobody. Don't make no difference who the guy

is, long's he's with you. I tell ya, I tell ya a guy gets too lonely
and he gets sick.

Man Alone

This is Steinbeck's portrait of Cain in the modern world, or
Man Alone, whose fate is so severe that he may feel compelled to echo the words of Cain to the Lord: "My punishment
is more than I can bear." In *Of Mice and Men* Steinbeck gives
us the case history of two simple mortals who try to escape
the homelessness, economic futility, and psychological soul-
corruption which Scripture embodies in the curse of Cain.

If in Scene One Lennie and George affirm their fraternity
openly and without embarrassment, in Scene Two George is
more hesitant. "He's my ... cousin," he tells the ranch boss.
"I told his old lady I'd take care of him." This is no betrayal
on George's part, but a cover-up required by the circumstances. For the boss is highly suspicious of the Lennie-
George fellowship. "You takin' his pay away from him?" he
asks George. "I never seen one guy take so much trouble for
another guy." A short time later Curley also sounds the note
of suspicion, extending it by a particularly nasty innuendo:
when George says "We travel together," Curley replies, "Oh,
so it's that way." Steinbeck is implying here the general response of most men towards seeing two individuals who
buddy around together in a friendless world where isolation
is the order of the day: there must be exploitation involved,
either financial or sexual! At the same time Steinbeck is developing the allegorical level of his story by suggesting that
the attitude of Cain ("I know not: Am I my brother's
keeper?") has become universal. Even the sympathetic and
understanding Slim expresses some wonder at the Lennie-
George fraternity. "Ain't many guys travel around together,"
Slim says in Scene Two. "I don't know why. Maybe ever'body
in the whole damned world is scared of each other." This
too, as Steinbeck interprets the Biblical story, is a part of
Cain's curse: distrust. Later on, in order to give the theme of
Aloneness another dimension, Steinbeck stresses the solitude of Crooks and Curley's wife, both of whom express a
craving for company and "someone to talk to."

Notwithstanding the fact that they are obviously swim-
ming against the current, Lennie and George continue to
reaffirm their solidarity all along, right up to and including
the last moments of Lennie's life in Scene Six. Here a big

rabbit, which Lennie in his disturbed state of mind has hallucinated, tells the half-wit fugitive that George is sick of him and is going to go away and leave him. "He won't," Lennie cries. "He won't do nothing like that. I know George. Me an' him travels together." Actually Steinbeck's novella advances and develops, ebbs and flows, around the basic image of the Lennie-George relationship. Almost all the characters react to it in one way or another as the successive scenes unfold. In Scenes One, Two, and Three, despite the discouraging opinions of outsiders, the companionship remains intact and unthreatened. Midway into Scene Three the partnership undergoes augmentation when Candy is admitted into the scheme to buy the little farm. Late in Scene Four Crooks offers himself as another candidate for the fellowship of soul-brothers and dreamers. This is the high point of optimism as regards the main theme of the story; this is the moment when a possible reversal of the curse of Cain seems most likely, as Steinbeck suggests that the answer to the Lord's question might be: Yes, I am my brother's keeper. If we arrive at this point with any comprehension of the author's purposes, we find ourselves brought up short by the idea: what if this George-Lennie-Candy-Crooks fraternity were to become universal!

TURNING POINT

But later in the same scene, the entrance of Curley's wife signals the turning point as the prospects for the idea of brotherhood-as-a-reality begin to fade and darken. As throughout the story she represents a force that destroys men and at the same time invites men to destroy her, as she will finally in Scene Five offer herself as a temptation which Lennie cannot resist, so in Scene Four Curley's wife sows the seeds that eventually disrupt the fellowship. Entering into the discussion in Crooks' room in the stable, she insults Crooks, Candy, and Lennie, laughs at their dream farm, and threatens to invent the kind of accusation that will get Crooks lynched. Crooks, reminded of his position of impotence in a white man's society, immediately withdraws his offer to participate in the George-Lennie-Candy farming enterprise. But Crooks' withdrawal, while extremely effective as social criticism, is much more. It represents an answer to the question Steinbeck is considering all along: is man meant to make his way alone or accompanied? Obviously this is one occasion, among many others in the story, when Steinbeck suggests the answer. Crooks' hope for fraternal living is short-lived. At the conclusion of the scene he sinks back into his Aloneness.

From this point on, even though the dream of fellowship on the farm remains active, the real prospects for its fulfillment decline drastically. In Scene Five, after George and Candy discover the lifeless body of Curley's wife, they both face the realization that the little farm is now unattainable and the partnership dissolved. Actually the plan was doomed to failure from the beginning; for fraternal living cannot long survive in a world dominated by the Aloneness, homelessness, and economic futility which Steinbeck presents as the modern counterpart of Cain's curse. Immediately following his discovery of Curley's wife's body, George delivers a speech that dwells on the worst possible aftermath of Lennie's misdeed; and this is not the wrath of Curley or the immolation of Lennie or the loss of the farm, but the prospect of George's becoming a Man Alone, homeless, like all the others and a victim as well of economic futility:

> I'll work my month an' I'll take my fifty bucks and I'll stay all night in some lousy cat house. Or I'll set in some poolroom til ever'body goes home. An' then I'll come back an' work another month an' I'll have fifty bucks more.

This speech represents the true climax of the novella, for it answers the question which is Steinbeck's main interest throughout. Now we know the outcome of the Lennie-George experiment in fellowship, as we know the Aloneness of man's essential nature. In subtle ways, of course, Steinbeck has been hinting at this conclusion all along, as for example in the seven references spaced throughout Scenes Two and Three to George's playing solitaire in the bunkhouse. For that matter the answer is implied in the very first line of the story when the author establishes his setting "A few miles south of Soledad . . . ," Soledad being at one and the same time a town in Central California and the Spanish word for solitude or aloneness.

But there are still other suggested meanings inherent in the dream farm and the failure of the dream. The plan is doomed not only because human fellowship cannot survive in the post-Cain world, but also because the image of the farm, as conceived by George and Lennie and Candy, is overly idealized, the probability being that life, even if they obtained the farm, would not consist of the comfort, plenty, and interpersonal harmony they envision. The fruits and vegetables in abundance, the livestock and domestic animals, and the community of people involved ("Ain't gonna be no more trouble. Nobody gonna hurt nobody nor steal from 'em")—these are impractical expectations. George and Lennie, who were to some extent inspired by questions growing out of the story of Cain in Chapter Four of Genesis, want to retreat to Chapter Two and live in Eden! Of all ambitions in a fallen world, this is possibly the most unattainable; for paradise is lost, as the name of Steinbeck's hero, George Milton, suggests. And though there will always be men like Candy, who represents sweet hope, the view of Crooks, who represents black despair, is probably a more accurate appraisal of the human condition: "Nobody never gets to heaven, and nobody gets no land. It's just in their head. They're all the time talkin' about it, but it's jus' in their head." Obviously in this context Crooks' comment about nobody ever getting land refers not to literal ownership, but to the dream of contentment entertained by the simple workmen who come and go on the ranch.

NAMES THAT START WITH *C*

Like William Goldhurst, Peter Lisca believes that in Of Mice and Men *Steinbeck is indeed painting a portrait of Cain in the modern world. In this excerpt from his book* John Steinbeck: Nature and Myth, *Lisca links* Of Mice and Men *to the Cain and Abel story by describing the biblical significance of each character's name.*

A . . . hint of the Biblical analogue lies in the preponderance of names beginning with *C*—Candy, Crooks, Carlson, Curley, Curley's wife (as she is always known). Furthermore, that there are no names beginning with *A* is in accord with the Biblical account that Abel had no descendants. Correspondingly, the scene is an agricultural one, and the workers, as migrants, fulfill God's "curse from the Earth" in the Old Testament: they are fugitives and vagabonds to whom the earth does "not yield her strength." Moreover, each of the *C* characters is in some way, and to varying degrees, a destroyer, even if only of a dream (Crooks) or of a dog (Candy).

Only one of the workers is an exception to this Cain identification—Whit (Wheat?), in whom we see no destructiveness, but who nevertheless is described as if bowed down by a sack

THE NATURE OF MAN

To pursue the Milton parallel a step further, we perceive immediately that Steinbeck has no intention of justifying the ways of God to man. On the contrary, if anything *Of Mice and Men* implies a critique of Hebrew-Christian morality, particularly in the area of the concept of punishment for sin. This opens up still another dimension of meaning in our interpretation of Steinbeck's novella. If George and Lennie fail to attain their dream farm (for reasons already explored), and the dream farm is a metaphor or image for heaven (as suggested by Crooks' speech in Scene Four) then the failure to achieve the dream farm is most likely associated with the question of man's failure to attain heaven. Steinbeck's consideration of this last-named theme is not far to seek. Along this particular line of thought, Lennie represents one essential aspect of man—the animal appetites, the craving to touch and feel, the impulse toward immediate gratification of sensual desires. George is the element of Reason which tries to control the appetites or, better still, to elevate them to a higher and more sublime level. As Lennie's hallucinatory rabbit advises him

---

of grain and thus figuratively associated with Cain. Of the four people mentioned but not present in the novel, two combine the *A* and *C* initials—Aunt Clara, Andy Cushman. Of the other two, both madams of whorehouses, the bad one is called Clara, but the "better" one, like Whit, has a name without the Cain initial—Suzy.

The names of the three main characters—George, Lennie, Slim—also avoid any use of the initial letters; yet Lennie kills Curley's wife, George kills his "brother," and Slim directs the killing of both Candy's dog and Lennie. Slim, through such attributes as his "understanding beyond thought," "God-like eyes," his "ageless"-ness, and his exercise of irrefutable authority, is clearly a God figure. He directs the necessary killing of Candy's dog, and of Lennie as well, out of love and compassion: the dog is old and suffering; it would be "no good" to have the vicious Curley kill Lennie, or to "lock him up an' strap him down and put him in a cage." George, too, kills out of knowledge and love. As for Lennie, Slim himself observes, "He ain't mean. . . . He's jes' like a kid. . . ." Lennie's killing of Curley's wife, as of the mice and puppies earlier in the book, is done out of some level of love, and in innocence.

near the conclusion: "Christ knows George done ever'thing
he could to jack you outa the sewer, but it don't do no good."
Steinbeck suggests throughout that the appetites and Reason
coexist to compose the nature of man. ("Me an' him travels
together.") He goes on to suggest that the effort to refine man
into something rare, saintly, and inhuman is another unattainable ambition. Even when Reason (George) manages to
communicate to the appetites (Lennie) its urgent message
("You crazy son-of-a-bitch. You keep me in hot water all the
time . . . I never get no peace.") the appetites are incapable of
satisfying Reason's demands. This submerged thesis is suggested when Aunt Clara—like the big rabbit, a product of
Lennie's disturbed imagination—scolds Lennie in Scene Six:

> "I tol' you an' tol' you. I tol' you, 'Min' George because he's
> such a nice fella an' good to you.' But you don't never take no
> care. You do bad things."
> And Lennie answered her, "I tried, Aunt Clara, ma'am. I
> tried and tried. I couldn' help it."

The animal appetites, even though well attended and well
intentioned, cannot be completely suppressed or controlled.
Thus, the best man can hope for is a kind of insecure balance of power between these two elements—which is in fact
what most of the ranch hands accomplish, indulging their
craving for sensual pleasure in a legal and commonplace
manner each payday. Failing this, man must suppress absolutely the appetites which refuse to be controlled, as
George does in the symbolic killing of Lennie at the conclusion of the novella. Possibly this is a veiled reference to the
drastic mutilation of man's nature required by the Hebrew-
Christian ethic. At the same time the theological implications of *Of Mice and Men* project the very highest regard for
the noble experiment in fraternal living practiced by George
and Lennie; and possibly the time-scheme of their stay on
the ranch—from Friday to Sunday—is a veiled reference to
the sacrifice of Christ. He too tried to reverse the irreversible
tide of Cain's curse by serving as the ultimate example of
human brotherhood.

At this point without, I hope, undue emphasis, we might
attempt to answer some specific objections which have
been raised by critics of *Of Mice and Men*. The faults most
often cited are the pessimism of Steinbeck's conclusion,
which seems to some readers excessive; and the author's attempt to impose a tragic tone upon a story which lacks

characters of tragic stature. Both of these censures might be accepted as valid, or at least understood as reasonable, if we read the novella *on the surface level of action and character-development.* But a reading which takes into account the mythical-allegorical significance of these actions and characters not only nullifies the objections, but opens up new areas of awareness. For example, although Lennie and George are humble people, without the status of traditional tragic characters, their dream is very much like the dream of Plato for an ideal Republic. And their experiment in fellowship is not at all different from the experiment attempted by King Arthur. And at the same time it is reminiscent of at least one aspect of Christ's ministry. These are remote parallels to *Of Mice and Men,* yet they are legitimate and lend some measure of substance, nobility, and human significance to Steinbeck's novella. Its pessimism is not superimposed upon a slight story, as charged, but has been there from the opening line, if we know how to read it. Furthermore, the pessimism is not inspired by commercialism or false theatrics, but by the Hebrew Testament. ("And Cain said unto the Lord, My punishment is greater than I can bear.")

A COMPLEX STORY

But let us tie up our loose ends, not with reference to critics, but with a brief summary of our discoveries during this investigation. *Of Mice and Men* is a realistic story with life-like characters and a regional setting, presented in a style highly reminiscent of stage drama. Steinbeck's technique also includes verbal ambiguity in place names and character names, *double entendre* in certain key passages of dialogue, and a mythical-allegorical drift that invites the reader into areas of philosophical and theological inquiry. Sources for the novella are obviously Steinbeck's own experience as a laborer in California; but on the allegorical level, *Of Mice and Men* reflects the early chapters of the Book of Genesis and the questions that grow out of the incidents therein depicted. These consist primarily of the consideration of man as a creature alone or as a brother and companion to others. In addition Steinbeck's story suggests the futility of the all-too-human attempt to recapture Eden, as well as a symbolic schema which defines human psychology. Steinbeck also implies a critique of the Hebrew-Christian ethic, to the effect that the absolute suppression of the animal appetites misrepresents the reality of human experience.

Finally we should say that Steinbeck's emphasis, on both the allegorical and realistic levels, is on the nobility of his characters' attempt to live fraternally. Even though the experiment is doomed to failure, Steinbeck's characters, like the best men of every age, dedicate themselves to pursuing the elusive grail of fellowship.

The War Between Good and Evil

Leo Gurko

Leo Gurko was a professor of English at Hunter College until 1972. In his view *Of Mice and Men* represents the principles of a Manichean universe— a setting of perpetual combat between the realms of lightness and darkness, good versus evil. Into this primeval conflict enter George and Lennie, representing the reigning forces of light and dark, respectively. While both strive for the same goal, their very natures are irreconcilable. This paradox, according to Gurko, lies at the heart of both the novel and Steinbeck's vision of the cosmos.

Of the great religions, Manicheism generates the most suspense. In it, the contending principles of good and evil, God and Satan, light and darkness, soul and body are so evenly matched that for long periods darkness is actually triumphant over light. In Christianity, the rebellious angels rise up but are easily defeated in battle and contemptuously cast down into hell. One never gets the impression that Satan is a serious threat to God or that he has any real chance of prevailing. In Manicheism, he is not only a serious threat but for a time he actually does prevail. When God sends his agent, Primal Man, to put down darkness, Primal Man is defeated in battle and taken prisoner. Particles of light are captured by the nether forces and the realm of light itself driven back.

THE POWER OF DARKNESS

The idea of God in a state of defeat is extraordinarily dramatic. And unique. In other monotheistic religions, the triumph of God is not only ultimate but a priori [a given], and

Excerpted from Leo Gurko, "*Of Mice and Men*: Steinbeck as Manichean," *University of Windsor Review*, vol. 8, no. 2, Spring 1973. Reprinted by permission of the *University of Windsor Review*.

his defeat in any confrontation is all but inconceivable. The Christians *know* that God will conquer the Devil, and they know it in advance. The Moslems *know* that they will triumph over the infidels. The Jews *know* that the Messiah will come. In contrast, the Manicheans take a far darker view of things. They know that on any given occasion God *can* be beaten for in fact he already has been.

This first defeat leads to a second, equally grave. Adam and Eve are produced not by God but by the powers of darkness, and the cosmos on the human side, which is to be the next great arena, is initiated and in its early stages dominated by these powers. The conviction that our first parents were demon-born rather than created by God in His own image lent Manicheism an especially sombre cast. Mani himself was fanatical on the issue of chastity. Sex is reserved to darkness. There is no sexual activity in the sphere of light. Light evokes. Darkness generates. Sex and body are associated with Eve, who is composed wholly of dark elements, while Adam has in his makeup particles of light. Fleshly intercourse and the begetting of children are evils from which men are to be rescued by a life of asceticism and renunciation. In the end, the great struggle for the universe is resumed and at last concluded: Primal Man is released, men are redeemed, the cosmos (having served its purpose as supreme battlefield) is dissolved, and the nether powers thrust back forever into the realm of darkness.

For self-evident reasons, Manicheism was branded as a heresy by other religions. But for a thousand years, from the third through the thirteenth centuries, it spread westward from Persia and exercised a pervasive and profound influence on Europe. Augustine himself was a Manichean for nine years before turning Christian. The emphasis of Manicheism on the power of fertility of darkness seemed closer to the facts of human experience than the more cheerful, perhaps even complacent mythology of other creeds. This may be one reason why it did not finally survive: its cosmology was too tragic and dangerous, its sexual demands too severe. But while not ultimately satisfactory, or satisfying, as religion, Manicheism is marvelously suited to drama. Nothing is more dramatic than a contest between two combatants of perfectly balanced strength, especially if the cosmos itself is divided between them. And it is on the dramatic side that Manicheism has made its great appeal to modern literature. . . .

The Manichean element, . . . is visible in Steinbeck's work from the start, but it is not until *Of Mice and Men,* written when Steinbeck was at the height of his powers, that it becomes paramount. This celebrated little novel, wedged between *In Dubious Battle* and *The Grapes of Wrath,* wonderfully reveals Steinbeck in his Manichean aspect.

MIND AND BODY

The antagonists appear at once, and embody the warring Manichean principles of mind and body. They are of course George and Lennie, locked together in the same life process but ultimately irreconcilable, with one compelled to slay the other. Their linkage is indicated as they first appear by the common uniform they wear. "Both are dressed in denim trousers and in denim coats with brass buttons. Both wore black shapeless hats and both carried tight blanket rolls slung over their shoulders." The uniform suggests their shared activity. They are ranch hands, working the earth. They are also itinerants, involved not with a particular plot of ground but with everywhere. Even their dream of owning their own place has this omnipresent quality: it starts out as something in the sky, the pure product of their eager imaginations, then comes down to a specific section of ground with a previous owner and a price tag. The dream is both ideal and real—it extends over all the available ground. This element of universality, at once abstract and concrete, is one of the story's special qualities.

While George and Lennie are thus deeply joined, they are also profoundly separated. George "was small and quick, dark of face, with restless eyes and sharp, strong features. Every part of him was defined: small, strong hands, slender arms, a thin and bony nose. Behind him walked his opposite, a huge man, shapeless of face, with large, pale eyes, with wide, sloping shoulders; and he walked heavily, dragging his feet a little, the way a bear drags his paws. His arms did not swing at his sides, but hung loosely." Their separateness is emphasized by their walking in single file, "and even in the open one stayed behind the other." George has a small body and a big brain, Lennie has a huge physique and a tiny brain. These deliberate polarities strain our belief in them as individual figures, but are absolutely necessary to establish them as reigning forces in the Manichean struggle for the world. The paradox of their existence is that they are at once partners and enemies. They strive for the same goal while destined by their natures to split apart. It is a paradox that lies both at the heart of the novel and Steinbeck's vision of the cosmos.

LENNIE: A CREATURE OF DARKNESS

Sex, embodied in Curley's wife, is associated with what she calls "the big guy," i.e. Lennie. George seems apart from it, and even when he speaks of going to a brothel, he has as little interest in it as getting drunk. George is sober, chaste, almost monastic in his habits. Lennie, in contrast, is uncontrollably sensuous. His whole being seems concentrated in his hands. He doesn't *see* anything very clearly, being a creature of darkness; touch is the focus of his energies. He picks up and tosses recordbreakingly heavy bales of barley. In the fight with Curley, it is Curley's hand that he crushes. He loves to stroke rabbits and mice, and to run his hands over women's hair and silk dresses. But his touch is deadly, and in the end he kills everything he touches. He doesn't mean to; his actions derive not from any centre of moral or psychological individuality but from his existence as a mindless, overwhelming force. As a force, he draws no distinction between life and death. He extracts as much pleasure in stroking a dead mouse as a live one.

Despite their radical dissimilarity, George feels obligated to "save" Lennie. In this he has a sense of almost religious mission. He grumbles about it throughout the novel. He is forever ragging Lennie about what a nuisance he is and how much happier he, George, would be if he could somehow be rid of him. But all this is on the surface. George feels deeply compelled to control Lennie. They were both born in the same town and Lennie was turned over to him as a family responsibility. But it is more than a legacy from the past. George finds the task personally gratifying. It is of course gratifying to his ego; no one can resist the temptation of being the master of some one else's destiny. It also heightens the quality of his own life. As Warren French theorized, George is rescued from dullness and mediocrity by maneuvering to keep Lennie out of trouble. And George has his hands full throughout. Lennie is his charge but also an immense counterweight pulling him constantly toward destruction. As the story opens, they have just narrowly escaped being lynched in Weed, where Lennie got into one of his "episodes" with a young girl. George, fearing the worst, prepares Lennie for his next "escape," and the first chapter ends on this note of foreboding. Life with Lennie is complicated and dangerous; it can all blow up at any moment, and it is not just their jobs and their livelihood that are at stake, but their lives. The novel, in its immediate as well as larger implications, is literally a matter of life and death.

The cosmological element is further highlighted by the fact that both George and Lennie are killers. They assume the right to impose death as though they were gods, and this raises them beyond the mortal. George is conscious and calculating, so he shoots Lennie consciously and calculatingly. Lennie is spontaneous and irrational, so he kills mice, puppies, rabbits, and Curley's wife unintentionally and irrationally. These awesome acts are the same for each; they flow naturally and quite unimpededly from the center of their beings. Steinbeck's approach to them, persistent throughout his work, is to establish their surface authenticity, pass over and indeed deliberately ignore their psychological insides, and settle finally upon their role as forces in nature. Readers who demand attention to the psychological contours of the individual self, who regard the characterization developed so magnificently in the nineteenth-century novel as the norm of fiction, will inevitably find *Of Mice and Men* sentimental and pretentious: sentimental because it arouses emotions and emotional responses too large for the simply drawn characters to sustain; pretentious because it imposes upon a pair of ragged, marginal itinerant laborers, one of whom is a virtual idiot, the tragic struggle of nothing less than the universe itself.

OF MICE AND MEN AS PARABLE

If, however, Steinbeck's source is not the modern novel but the ancient parable—or the early epic, which is a kind of large-framed, fleshed-out parable—*Of Mice and Men* can be read as a peculiarly contemporary example of the genre. It is Steinbeck's Manichean parable, as *The Grapes of Wrath,* following it immediately in order of composition, is his Christian one. But the parable, while it eschews psychological embroidery and complexity of characterization, depends very much on surface credibility, on the authentic rendering of appearance, gesture, and word. And here even his harshest critics must concede Steinbeck's mastery. His ranch hands, whether communing in the bunkhouse or sweating in the field, look, sound, feel, even smell like what they are supposed to be. Their dialogue, credible enough in terms of grammatical construction, elision, monosyllabic diction, and colloquial nuance, is entirely free of any trace of abstraction, of that tendency to abandon the physical for the metaphysical that has tainted so much "uneducated" speech and dialect from [William] Wordsworth to [William] Saroyan.

Even the refrain—the most formal device in evidence here—suggests the epic. At Lennie's urging, George recites the tale of their Promised Land: the little farm they will own some day, where Lennie can tend his rabbits and they will be rid of all their troubles. There they will be owners rather than workers and no one can throw them out. They will work only when they feel like it and loaf when so inclined. Their aimless, homeless wandering will come to an end, and eternal bliss will set in. Like an ancient scop or medieval troubadour, George relates this beautiful dream as though it were a chant or an orison: "He repeated his words rhythmically as though he had said them many times before." He has a rapt audience of one, Lennie, sometimes two, Lennie and Candy. Like a congregation caught up in ritual prayer, Lennie breaks in at set intervals with his own aria: "Tell about that place, George." "We could live offa the fatta the lan'." "An' rabbits. An' I'd take care of 'em. Tell how I'd do that." And George would tell. He would be so caught up in his own telling that he would soar off into the empyrean. "George sat entranced with his own picture." The effect of all this—the chant, the dream, the repetitious rhythm, the enraptured teller and his spellbound audience lifted ecstatically out of themselves—is to blur the individual moment and universalize the event. The impression conveyed is that this sort of thing has been going on, in no very different terms, since the beginning of time. Even *Of Mice and Men*'s original title, "Something That Happened," strengthens this impression by its deliberately toneless and impersonal anonymity.

PLAY FORMAT

The movement from the particular to the general is accelerated by Steinbeck's well-advertised intention of constructing his story like a play. Description is condensed. The cast of characters is stripped to its minimal impulses. Elaboration of any kind is forgone. The six separate chapters are treated as though they were acts on stage: related to one another, to be sure, in terms of advancing movement, but deliberately fashioned as autonomous, self-contained units with an existence of their own as distinct from their existence in the novel as a whole. They are divided neatly into three locales: chapters one and six take place by the river, two and three in the bunkhouse, four and five in the barn. This 1 2-2 3-3 1 arrangement is designed for concentration—each locale appears twice—and for climax: the return at the end to the scene of the beginning. In its simplicity, leanness, and brevity, it seeks to reduce everything to essentials, even to quintessentials. There is no room for commentary or nuance, none for the intricate machinery of the modern novel. Steinbeck's instinct has always been for a return to early forms of literature: the drama, the epic, and the parable. *Of Mice and Men* is his supreme combination of all these.

CHROMATIC SCHEME

The lighting scheme of the novel supports its dramatic intentions. The prevailing atmosphere is a half-light shading toward darkness, precisely suited to the Manichean setting where the agents of God are always descending to do battle with the dark forces. In the opening chapter we are out-of-doors by the river, with evening falling. We then move indoors to the two scenes in the bunkhouse. The first of these takes place in the morning, with the sun filtering through one of the side windows, leaving most of the room in shadow. The second is at night. The bunkhouse has a single, tin-shaded electric light in its centre, illuminating the table where the men sit, talk, and play cards. Away from this light the room grows progressively darker and the bunks along the walls are almost entirely in the dark. The scene shifts in the fourth and fifth chapters to the greater, more profound darkness of the barn. The animals are quartered there, and so is a single human being, the black man Crooks, the crippled stable buck who lives in the harness room. Though he longs to be with the others, racial discrimination makes this impossible, and his descent in both the physical and social spheres is symbolized by his deformity. This, and his blackness, root him appropriately in the novel's deepest level of descent.

The two barn sequences are also divided between darkness and day, reversing the order of the bunkhouse chapters.

Chapter four unfolds in Crooks' shed at night. Again the chiaroscuro [treatment of light and dark] is pronounced: "A small electric globe threw a meager yellow light," leaving most of the room in darkness. Chapter five takes place during the afternoon in the main section of the barn. "The afternoon sun sliced in through the cracks of the barn walls and lay in bright lines on the hay." Lennie has left George, left Crooks, and is now alone with the animals in the sub-human world of the stable. Here, with the light and darkness splintered into alternating strips, the murder of Curley's wife triggers the sombre tragedy of the final chapter. Her unpremeditated death leads to the premeditated death of Lennie, back in the outer air by the river. The refrain motif of the story reaches its chromatic climax with the falling afternoon light on the last scene, on its way to completing the circle that began at the same point with the falling light on the opening pages. It is the interpenetration of light and dark, with each given an exactly similar weight and place with the other, that powerfully reinforces the Manichean idea that these contending cosmic forces are, until all but the very end of their struggle, of equal strength.

GEORGE: A CREATURE OF LIGHT

The smaller linkages of the book are similarly suggestive. Lennie is always associated with enclosures: weeds, caves, barns, kennels, hutches, stalls. George wishes at one point he could just put him in a cage; Slim warns that society *will* put him in a cage. George alerts Lennie to hide in the brush in case of trouble. In his domestic quarreling with George, Lennie threatens to run off to the hills and sulk in a cave. In the bunkhouse he spends most of his time lying on his bunk, only dimly visible, at times with his face turned to the wall. George is forever urging and cautioning him to stay out of sight, to say nothing and be as inconspicuous as possible. If Lennie is wholly a night creature, George is linked with the processes and artifacts of light. "The rims of his eyes were red with sun glare." In the bunkhouse he is seen at the table in the center, with the electric light shining upon him or catching the rays of the sun. Except for a brief moment when he looks at the body of Lennie's last victim, he never enters the barn. In gesture, physique, speech, he is clearly and sharply defined, in contrast to Lennie's shapelessness. George is also bathed throughout in intellectual light, his judgments and responses emerging without exception in lucid silhouette. One *feels* the powerful, inchoate presence of Lennie. George one *sees*. . . .

The supporting characters in *Of Mice and Men* are a grab bag of the ordinary human world, the world which is in Mani's terms the final scene of the cosmological conflict. The elements in each are deliberately mixed. Curley's wife is the Manichean Eve, the purely sexual temptress who brings nothing but trouble to the surrounding males. But she is humanized by her unhappiness, and the story of her young life with its banal dream of Hollywood success and its painful frustrations, which she reveals to Lennie just before he kills her, has a redeeming, even softening pathos drama-tized by her features in death: "And the meanness . . . and the discontent and the ache for attention were all gone from her face. She was very pretty and simple, and her face was sweet and young. Now her rouged cheeks and her reddened lips made her seem alive and sleeping very lightly." Curley him-self seems wholly a creature of darkness, a vicious stunted figure seeking to compensate for his lack of sexual potency by training himself as a boxer and beating up helpless men bigger than himself. Yet he, too, is emotionally vulnerable, humanized in turn by his abnormal capacity to feel pain, by his feverishly hypersensitive reaction to those around him.

Each of the others bears within himself some splinter of light. Candy, old, worn, and on the edge of senility, sum-mons the energy to link himself with George and Lennie's dream. Crooks accepts his black humiliation, bows before the white man's contempt and the white woman's threat, yet his capacity to swallow insult and submit to his own degra-dation is balanced by a penetrating intelligence: he analyzes and understands his situation with total clarity. Carlson chills us with his proposal to shoot Candy's aging dog; still, someone has to do the dirty work, and it is appropriate that, later, George should dispatch Lennie with Carlson's gun. There is one figure who approaches an ideal standard: Slim, the expert mule-skinner, the supremely skilful workingman, invested with superhuman qualities. Yet if he is a god, he is a curiously ineffectual one, commenting on events but un-able to control or channel them. He is a sympathetic judge of George's dilemma. "You hadda, George. I swear you hadda," he comforts him at the end, but he is quite unable to prevent anyone from doing what his nature compels him to.

The moral equations are similarly mixed. In the novel,

virtue nearly always leads to disaster. Lennie loves puppies and mice, but succeeds only in killing them. Candy's faithful attachment to his old dog leaves him in a state of shock and grief at its death. George's feelings for Lennie, an intricate amalgam of brother, father, and keeper, force him to slay his friend. There is an impersonality, an inevitability about these poignant events that reflects the character of the larger world in which they occur. That larger world joins light and darkness at their points of maximum interfusion. On the human level, the novel joins the redeeming emotion and the tragic action at exactly the same point, the moment when they meld into one another with maximum force.

A WORLD OF LONERS

Perhaps the most suggestive dualism of the novel is its contrast between men who travel together and those who travel alone. There are many more of the second than the first. Those who travel together are indeed so rare that they arouse comment. The ranch boss thinks that George must be exploiting Lennie in some way, perhaps robbing him of his pay: "I never seen one guy take so much trouble for another guy. I just like to know what your interest is." Slim, naturally, takes a more philosophical view: "Ain't many guys travel around together. . . . I don't know why. Maybe ever'-body in the whole damned world is scared of each other." The Negro, for whom the problem of connecting with others is peculiarly hard, sees his own need reflected in George and Lennie: "I seen it over an' over—a guy talkin' to another guy and it don't make no difference if he don't hear or understand. The thing is, they're talkin', or they're settin' still not talkin'. . . . George can tell you screwy things, and it don't matter. It's just the talking. It's just bein' with another guy."

All the loners are drawn to the pair that are together. Candy wants to buy into their farm. So does Crooks. Slim is attracted to George, and goes off with him after Lennie's death. Curley's wife attaches herself to Lennie, and so in his curiously belligerent fashion does Curley. His atrocious assault upon Lennie, from which he emerges with a crushed hand, establishes a kind of brutal intimacy between them. This theme of human beings who are linked and those who are atomized, like the other themes of the novel, subtly underlines its Manichean character. The dark, psychologically disturbed figures—Curley, Curley's wife, Crooks—are drawn into Lennie's orbit. The one man drawn to George is Slim, endowed throughout with godlike attributes: "He moved with a majesty only achieved by royalty and master crafts-men.... There was a gravity in his manner and a quiet so profound that all talk stopped when he spoke. His authority was so great that his word was taken on any subject.... His speech had overtones... of understanding beyond thought." "George looked over at Slim and saw the calm, God-like eyes fastened on him."

A MANICHEAN VISION

Underlying the novel, and controlling it, is Steinbeck's vision of the universe as the scene of a decisive and unpredictable encounter of immense forces. It is this vision that gives *Of Mice and Men* its quality as a parable, makes it seem larger than the life it describes, and frees the characters from the sentimentality into which they would obviously sink if taken on their own literal, limitedly human terms. And the vision is essentially Manichean. Lennie and George are fated by their very natures to be joined in extraordinary intimacy and irreconcilable hostility. Moreover, the darkness represented by Lennie is just as "creative" and potent as George's light. George may be the executor of the dream, but it is Lennie who conceives it. It is George's incantatory voice that gives it verbal shape, but it is Lennie whom it lifts to ecstatic heights. And the dependence of one upon the other is total in both human and cosmic terms. Lennie and George are in-dispensable to one another as Manichean darkness and light are, and in exactly the same way.

It is true of Steinbeck... that Manichean psychology and drama are separated from its ethics and theology. The good-bad sides of God and Satan, the ultimate triumph of one over the other, an apocalyptic event accompanied by the dissolu-tion of human history, are of little interest to these modern writers. They concentrate instead on what is visible and ver-ifiable: The contending forces govern and shape our des-tinies. Both are equally potent and powerful sources of life. They are indispensable to one another while remaining ir-reconcilable, and the outcome of their perpetual combat is beyond prediction.

Of these ideas and visions, *Of Mice and Men*—lean, small-boned, delicately framed—is a supple and effective embodiment.

Misogyny in *Of Mice and Men*

Jean Emery

In this feminist reading, Jean Emery argues that *Of Mice and Men* is a chronicle of society's injustice to women. She describes the bunkhouse as a patriarchal world in which the players attempt to eliminate all vestiges of femininity. In her analysis, Lennie and George personify the stereotypical attributes of femininity and masculinity. Lennie is docile, submissive, and dependent; George is his protector. In choosing to kill Lennie, Emery concludes, George chooses masculinity over femininity, confirming the novel's message that a partnership integrating both traits is doomed.

Of Mice and Men is not, as most critics would have us believe, a poignant, sentimental drama of an impossible friendship and an unattainable dream. Rather, the story actually demonstrates the achievement of a dream—that of a homogeneous male fraternity not just to repress, but to eliminate women and femininity. *Of Mice and Men* depicts the rescue of men from women, "a melodrama of beset manhood," to use the words of Nina Baym.

Textual evidence suggests that John Steinbeck, as chronicler of America's social inequities, intended *Of Mice and Men* as a critique of our society's most fundamental injustice. George and Lennie represent the duality of masculinity and femininity, their partnership a kind of marriage. Ultimately, George's need and desire to confirm his membership in the powerful and dominant male community drives him to kill his partner as a sacrificial rite of initiation. Bolstered by smaller, less dramatic, but nonetheless significant sacrifices, the text illustrates the insidious presence of this practice in our culture at large. That for more than 50 years

From Jean Emery, "Manhood Beset: Misogyny in *Of Mice and Men*," *San Jose Studies*, vol. 18, Winter 1992. Reprinted by permission of the author.

literary critics have read the text purely as an exposé of a failed *economic* dream corroborates a blindness to this issue and complicity in preserving the patriarchy.

George and Lennie as a couple display the stereotypical attributes of husband and wife. Lennie's refrain, "I got you to look after me, and you got me to look after you," solemnizes a kind of marriage vow between them. "We got a future," George says in reply. The glue that binds George and Lennie is the dream of a house and a couple of acres where they can "live off the fatta the lan'." George, the masculine creator of this dream, gives it voice and grounds it in the realm of possibility. But it is "feminine" Lennie who nurtures it and keeps it alive with his boundless obsession for hearing George tell it "like you done before."

As in many traditional marriages, this is not a partnership of equals but one of lord and vassal, owner and owned. George as the patriarch makes the decisions, controls the finances, decides where they'll work and live, dictates the conditions of the relationship ("no rabbits" is the threat employed), even regulates when Lennie can and cannot speak. Yet George wants power without the burden of responsibility. "God, you're a lot of trouble," he says more than once to Lennie. "I could get along so easy and so nice if I didn't have you on my tail."

George's droning retelling of the dream is done primarily for Lennie's benefit. George's own dream is really something quite different: "If I was alone I could live so easy. I could go get a job an' work, an' no trouble. No mess at all, and when the end of the month come I could take my fifty bucks and go into town and get whatever I want." The latent message, of course, is that life would be better without the complications of a relationship of a dependent "other."

POWER ISSUES

Relationships in this story center on the issue of power: who will have it and who will not. Obsessed with his ability to control Lennie's behavior (just as Curley is driven to regulate his wife's), George admonishes Lennie for carrying dead mice in his pocket, for directly responding to a question from the Boss, for bringing a pup into the bunkhouse. Such power frightens and, at the same time, thrills George. "Made me seem God damn smart alongside him," George tells Slim. "Why he'd do any damn thing I tol' him. If I tol' him to walk over a cliff, over he'd go." George then recounts the time Lennie nearly drowned demonstrating exactly such obedience.

Peter Lisca suggests that George needs Lennie as a rationalization for his own failure. But George's failure is not just his inability to establish his own autonomy. It is also his struggle to assure himself of his own masculinity and reject the disturbing influence of such feminine traits as gentleness, compassion, submissiveness, and weakness. Lennie's size and strength, a constant reminder of George's own physical puniness, presents a constant threat to George's vulnerable masculinity, clearly displayed in Lennie's effortless emasculation of Curley when Lennie crushes the bully's hand.

Demonstrations of masculinity suffuse the text. The ranch George and Lennie come to work—a stronghold of physical effort, rationality, and orderliness—reeks with maleness. The bunkhouse, utilitarian and void of decoration except for "those Western magazines ranch men love to read and scoff at and secretly believe," exemplifies the heroic male struggle to control nature, other men, and, inevitably, women.

Woman and, correspondingly, feminine traits are intruders and threats to this world, "entrappers" and "domesticators" in Baym's words, woman as temptress thwarting man in his journey of self-discovery and definition.

THE SEXUAL SNARE

In the novel some of the central female figures are the whores, who use their sexual powers to seduce men, robbing them of their financial stake. Women are poison, George tells us, "jailbait on a trigger." George and Lennie's dream, one all the men subscribe to in some measure, is, not surprisingly, devoid of women. The female taint precipitates the pathetic destruction of Lennie and, invariably, the ruination of every man's dream.

Curley's wife, the evil, disloyal seductress, personifies the "fallen" woman. She flaunts her sexuality (her only effective weapon in this arena), dressing like a bordello whore—heavy makeup, painted fingernails, red ostrich feathers on her slippers. She triggers the story's tragic events and George foresees this. "Been any trouble since she got here?" he asks.

Curley's wife (the only woman appearing in the story aside from the spectral Aunt Clara), is, in fact, so antagonistic to this environment that she remains nameless. She's called "tease," "tramp," "tart," "rat-trap," "jailbait," "bitch," "Curley's wife"—identity always contingent upon her relationship to men. By refusing to speak her name, these men attempt to rob her of her power over them, just as a superstitious and primitive native might refuse to invoke the name of a feared spirit.

George's reaction to her is particularly intriguing, since his vehemence seems vastly out of proportion to her possible influence on his life. "I seen 'em poison before, but I never seen no piece of jail bait worse than her." George clearly doesn't trust or even like women; to him they are liars and manipulators like the girl in Weed who cries rape when Lennie clutches at her dress. Curley's wife threatens the same action when Crooks and Candy try to throw her out of Crooks's room.

The essential conflict of the story—the strength of the bond between George and Lennie—hinges upon this desire for a world without the contaminating female. Lennie, despite his size, possesses characteristics traditionally identified as feminine; and his continued habitation of the male sphere eventually becomes intolerable for everyone, including George.

Stereotypically feminine, docile and submissive, dependent and lacking in self-assertiveness, Lennie obeys George like a good woman. "Baffled, unknowingly powerful, utterly will-less, he can not move without a leader," observes Harry Thornton Moore. Lennie is a pleaser, seeking approval, desiring love. We first see him mimicking George's behavior, a conscious ploy to endear himself to his protector. Lennie loves soft, sensual objects: mice, puppies, silky curls. He possesses maternal cravings, revealed in his affection for small animals. And playing into long-held prejudices against women's intelligence, Steinbeck makes Lennie a half-wit.

Lennie's superhuman strength does not contradict this interpretation of him as a feminine figure, but rather confirms it. Throughout history, taboos surrounding virginity, menstruation, and sexual intercourse have expressed men's dread of female sexuality. Images such as *vagina dentata* exemplify men's inordinate fear of submitting to a force that is unseen, uncontrollable, and menacing to their essential nature—"a generalized dread of women," in Freud's assessment: "The man is afraid of being weakened by the woman, infected with her femininity and of then showing himself incapable."

George displays mistrust, disgust, and barely disguised rage on the topic of women. He seems particularly to resent the shackles of his promise to Aunt Clara to care for Lennie (a vow, notably, given to a woman).

RESCUE FROM WOMEN

Of Mice and Men's solution to this strangling bind is the rescue of men by men from the grip of women. Freud, of course, vigorously promoted the significance of a boy's separation from his mother in achieving his sense of masculinity. Here the struggle manifests itself in the creation of what anthropologists call "men's house institutions." These cultural centers of male ritual and values ensure male solidarity and the overall segregation of the sexes within the tribal group. Any breach of house norms meets with severe censure and even social ostracism.

Sexual segregation is *de rigueur* on the ranch. "You ain't wanted here," Candy hisses at Curley's wife when she invades Crooks's room. Curley's wife and Lennie are excluded from the male rituals of card games, trips to town, and horseshoe tournaments. But then, so too are Crooks and Candy, despite their possession of the correct biological anatomy.

Crooks is ostracized because of race, a nonconformity to the norms of the tribal group. Candy's case is more complicated. His strength and usefulness are on the wane. He has been crippled, hence he is less of a man. More importantly, however, he fails to uphold the standards of desired male behavior. Just as his muscle has withered, Candy's emotional state has grown soft and sentimental. Male power demands a code of behavior that asserts control over property and possessions, whether they be wife or dog. Sentiment and attachment—dare one mention love—is of no consequence. Candy's dog is too old and feeble for work and has a "bad stink" to boot. But Candy can not bring himself to perform his manly duty of ridding himself of this no-longer-useful appendage. Carlson, rational, cold-hearted, eminently practical, the antithesis of femininity, takes on the job himself, in the process sealing Candy's expulsion from the male community.

LESSON FOR GEORGE

The lesson is not lost on George. When the crisis comes and Lennie is no longer "manageable," George, like a rancher suddenly confronted with a pet dog that has taken to killing sheep, follows Carlson's example, right down to shooting Lennie in the very spot Carlson marked on the dog's head. George's killing of Lennie is, in effect, his sacrificial rite of initiation into the male enclave.

By his action, George chooses virility over compassion, masculinity over femininity. Stoic, calm, and nearly emotionless, George's behavior, unlike Candy's, is manly. His lie about the actual events of Lennie's death, which on the surface suggests deep-felt emotion, actually serves to enhance his own male stature: diminutive George wrestling the giant, bone-crushing brute, Lennie, for a loaded Luger—and winning, getting off a clean shot to the back of the neck like a skilled marksman—a narrative straight out of a Western pulp magazine. Slim's proposal to go into town for a drink validates George's membership in the clubhouse. "Ya hadda, George. I swear you hadda."

By murdering Lennie, George rids himself of the very thing that sets himself apart from other men. Without Lennie, he is no longer a curiosity, a man of questionable masculinity because he travels with another. The demise of Lennie is also the demise of the dream. George thus establishes his solidarity with the other men for whom the dream will remain just talk.

Lennie's death need not necessarily mean the end of the dream, however. After all, Candy is still eager to pursue it. But partnership with Candy requires a different kind of relationship than the one George had with Lennie; and unwilling to reestablish a new hierarchy of dominator and dominated, one where George is not so obviously superior, he quickly abandons the dream.

What really stands in the way of the dream, however, is George's inability to accept the implied responsibility of the dream: shared contact with another—equal—human being. As Louis Owens writes, "It is Lennie's need for contact with other living beings, a craving the men of this world deny, that brings about his destruction." George, of course, is the instrument of this destruction and the ultimate judge of its validity. The inherent message of the text is that a partnership based on mutual caring and respect is doomed and the model of marrying masculine with feminine is by nature destructive and tragic. Ironically, while the masculine world despises female dependence and submissiveness, membership in the male community in fact rejects the possibility of true independence and autonomy.

The melodrama of beset manhood neatly rescues the men on this Salinas Valley ranch from the entrappers and domesticators. By story's end, all vestiges of femininity have been eliminated—Lennie, Curley's wife, Candy's dog, Lennie's mice and rabbits, even the deer that bound silently across the path through the willows to the pool; a path, it should be noted, "beaten hard by boys" and men.

Despite the prevailing belief that this story portrays the pathos of the quest for the American dream, the foregoing evidence suggests that *Of Mice and Men* is a Steinbeckian condemnation of the American male's inability to accommodate diversity and nonconformity, a terse commentary on misplaced values.

Carlson and Slim epitomize this conflict between domination and compassion. Warren French notes that Carlson is insensitive and brutal; Slim, kindly and perceptive. There is no sentiment in Carlson, an eminently practical, albeit destructive man. Curley's wife and Lennie, like Candy's dog, are to Carlson useless, intrusive, and annoying. A man of action, Carlson does not let emotional weakness keep him from doing what a man's got to do. His having the last word in the story—"Now what the hell ya suppose is eating them two guys?"—attests to the weight given the text's masculine message.

SLIM'S CHARACTERIZATION

The characterization of Slim, however, suggests some slight hope for reconciliation between male and female components and saves the text from a completely cynical misogyny. Slim is androgynous, what Carolyn Heilbrun defines as "a condition under which the characteristics of the sexes, and the human impulses expressed by men and women, are not rigidly assigned." Kindly, perceptive, compassionate, tender, intuitive, Slim is described in feminine terms. Even his hands are lean, delicate and as graceful as a temple dancer. "His ear heard more than was said to him, and his slow speech had overtones of thought, but of understanding beyond thought." Yet his feminine traits are coupled with images of virility. "His authority was so great that his word was taken on any subject, be it politics or love." He is "the prince of the ranch, capable of driving ten, sixteen, even twenty mules with a single line to the leader." Physically strong, powerful and in control, the others take their cue from Slim, who combines the finest attributes of male and female.

When he finds George and Lennie beside the pool, Slim perceptively recognizes George's internal struggle. He soothes George as a woman might; and yet, unlike a woman, he instructs George as to what he must do next, what "story" he must tell. The two leave together, as George and Lennie first arrived, a couple. *This* partnership may be different. Slim, the only character to integrate the masculine and feminine attributes of his own nature, may well influence the man who has so forcefully denied this integration.

A COMPASSIONATE PORTRAIT OF FEMININITY

Steinbeck's sympathy clearly lies with the feminine. Lennie tugs at a reader's heart in the same way that a child or defenseless animal might. So, too, his portrayal of Curley's wife in death softens earlier, viperous images of her: "And the meanness and the plannings and the discontent and the ache for attention were all gone from her face. She was very pretty and simple, and her face was sweet and young."

But most revealing of Steinbeck's attitude toward the material is a simple image he creates in the opening pages, one that becomes a metaphor for the text. Shortly before we meet George and Lennie, "a big carp rose to the surface of the pool, gulped air and then sank mysteriously into the dark water again, leaving widening rings on the water." If Steinbeck had intended our sympathy to lie with the status quo, the fish that rises to the surface would have been something other than a carp—a rainbow trout or a cut-throat perhaps, game fish known as strong, wiley fighters. Instead Steinbeck gives us the carp, a sucker fish, an invader that eventually takes over a pond or stream, muddying the waters and irrevocably altering the environment it penetrates. Smaller, weaker, and less aggressive species are quickly subsumed. Diversity can not be accommodated once the carp arrives. Over time, all except the carp disappear. The pond is no longer a very interesting or "wild" place. It is ruined.

"Violence without tragedy; that is the weakness of this book," writes Moore. "Sentimental," say others, dismissing the work as minor. The dictionary tells us sentimental means "influenced more by emotion than reason; acting from feeling rather than from practical and utilitarian motives." In short, feminine.

Steinbeck's carp, the men of the Salinas Valley, eliminate diversity and complexity out of a fear for their own survival. They huddle like a school of fish in their bunkhouse, confidence in their own self-definition residing in the absence of contrasting existences. They reign homogeneous, unvarying, sterile—big fish in ever-dwindling ponds.

CHAPTER 2

Symbols, Structure, and Fictional Method

READINGS ON

OF MICE AND MEN

Christian Symbolism in *Of Mice and Men*

Lee Dacus

In Lee Dacus's interpretation, *Of Mice and Men* contains symbols that parallel traditional Christian theology. Foremost, Lennie represents a Christian figure. As with a traditional Christian, Lennie maintains his faith in a dream of heaven—a little farm with rabbits—while he tries, futilely, to "obey" the rules. As Lennie's guide and protector, then, George serves as the Christ figure who not only keeps Lennie from harm but also, in a merciful, Christlike manner, serves as the instrument of his death.

Perhaps the greatest appeal of John Steinbeck's Lennie in *Of Mice and Men* comes from the fact that this character is cast as the traditional Christian figure worthy of the pen of [seventeenth-century English preacher and allegorist John] Bunyan. The echoes of this parallel, however, touch the reader as subtle overtones. And this writer admits to having read the novel more than once before this aspect of the author's meaning became apparent.

In this study of Lennie it is seen that, pure in heart but burdened with his great hulk of flesh to carry, he lumbers through life during the Great Depression crushing and killing, without intent, the things which please him or that he loves. Dreaming of his own special heaven, and trying to be obedient but unable to attain this, he, nevertheless, maintains his faith in his lord and master. In the final chapter, he dies looking across the river of his rendezvous with death (and George), unafraid, his dream of paradise before him.

If, then, Lennie serves as the Christian figure, we are forced to conclude that George, in the role of Lennie's only friend, his source of protection, aid, faith, and finally the instrument of his death, must stand, though much less well-defined, as the Christ figure.

From Lee Dacus, "Lennie as Christian in *Of Mice and Men*," *Southwest American Literature*, vol. 4 (1974), pp. 87-91. Reprinted by permission of *Southwest American Literature*.

Looking back to the beginning of the relationship of these two characters, it is discovered that when they were youngsters George had tormented Lennie in a most un-Christlike manner. His final act of mischief (which he confesses to the fatherly Slim) is committed as he tells Lennie to jump into the river to amuse a group of boys. Lennie almost drowned. George frantically pulls him from the water, resolving never to play another prank on his innocent friend. This is at least faintly reminiscent of Peter's abortive attempt to walk on the water at the invitation of Christ. After this incident George promised Lennie's Aunt Clara that he would look after her misfortunate nephew, which he did for the rest of Lennie's life in the manner of a Good Shepherd.

As the story opens, the reader finds the two friends walking wearily along a lonely, dusty road. In this scene George is verbally chastising Lennie for his transgressions. Lennie has stumbled into trouble in the town of Weed, and George has rescued him from an angry mob by hiding with him in the water of an irrigation ditch until they can make their escape in the night. This appears at a second glance to mirror the ritual of baptism. In the present scene, however, Lennie is pained by the displeasure of George and asks forgiveness, pleading to be told about the paradisical farm where George has promised that they will live (forever) and raise rabbits.

As they walk along, George discovers that Lennie is fondling a dead mouse which he is carrying in his jumper pocket. This may well represent the residue of dead sin which Christian yet carries about his person after regeneration; for his pleasure in stroking the mouse is exactly the same type of sin which almost lost him his life back in Weed. Lennie is punished and purified: George makes him reluctantly throw away the dead mouse and go in search of firewood. He brings back a few puny twigs and also, furtively, the carcass of the mouse. This entire scene very effectively illustrates the penitence of the Christian and the tendency of the flesh to return to the mortality of sin and death. The small quantity of firewood brought in by Lennie may also point up the inconsequentiality of Christian's works.

THE MOUSE AS SYMBOL

Lennie is again deprived of the mouse as George reads the guilt written on his face. Thus, the mouse becomes a complex symbol and foreshadowing device, signifying, at least, pleasure, sin, and death. But in addition to this, it constitutes a symbolic object in an important parallel: Even as the mouse's death is at the unintentional hands of Lennie who cared for it and wished it no ill, the death of Lennie is likewise at the hands of George who cared greatly for him and wished him only the best.

After George's exasperation has subsided, the two are preparing their supper at the fire on the river bank.

> Lennie still knelt. He looked off into the darkness across the river, "George, You want I should go away and leave you alone?"
>
> "Where the hell would you go?"
>
> . . . .
>
> "If you don' want me I can go off in the hills an' find a cave. I can go away any time."
>
> . . . .
>
> George said, "I want you to stay with me, Lennie. Jesus Christ, somebody'd shoot you for a coyote if you was by yourself. No, you stay with me . . ."

This scene is prayer-like in essence. The kneeling Lennie looks into the darkness of death across a river that seems ominous and offers to leave his friend if that is his will. The reply comes in the form of an impatient question: "Where the hell would you go?" This suggests that anywhere Lennie goes without George will be hell. The expletive George utters seems to be more significant than mere habit of speech: *"Jesus Christ,* somebody'd shoot you for a coyote." This is also an instance of sharp dramatic irony since it will be George who will do the shooting at last. "No, you stay with me," is uttered in the kindly tones of one who cares.

A little later, having forgotten George's impatience, Lennie begs to be told the story of the little farm they dream of. Finally George begins to talk in these words:

> "Guys like us, that work on ranches, are the loneliest guys in the world. They got no family. They don't belong no place . . . They ain't got nothing to look ahead to."
>
> Lennie was delighted. "That's it—That's it. Now tell how it is with us."
>
> George went on. "With us, it ain't like that. We got a future. We got somebody to talk to that gives a damn about us— —"
>
> Lennie broke in. "But not us! An' why? Because—because I got you to look after me, and you got me to look after you, and that's why."

As with the traditional Christian, Lennie's hope and delight is not in the present, but in the glorious future. George tells over again the promise of the farm, the pleasant evenings by the fire, and the endless and incomparable pleasures Lennie will enjoy feeding, tending, and playing with the (heavenly) rabbits. Finally, George admonishes Lennie in all gravity:

> "Well, look. Lennie—if you jus' happen to get in trouble like you always done before, I want you to come right here an' hide in the brush."
>
> "Hide in the brush," said Lennie slowly.
>
> "Hide in the brush 'till I come for you. Can you remember that?"
>
> "Sure I can, George. Hide in the brush 'till you come."

After they have rolled into their blankets beside the dying fire, Lennie calls to George and asks if they can have different-colored rabbits (Christian's idea of heaven is only limited by his imagination).

> "Sure," says George.
>
> "'Cause I can jus' as well go away, George, and live in a cave."
>
> "You can jus' as well go to hell," said George. "Shut up now."

The words of the retort were different, but the tone might have been the same as in "Thou shalt have no other gods before Me."

Later at the ranch, except for the fight with Curley, which might well symbolize Christian's struggle with Satan, Lennie mainly stays clear of trouble through the watchful protection of George, until the fatal scene in the barn out of George's sight in which Lennie kills the girl. This is through no intent but merely a product of childlike excitability and tremendous physical strength. Sensing that he is in deep trouble, Lennie makes his way to the spot along the river bank where he had promised to hide and wait for George.

A DEED OF LOVE

George, realizing that Lennie's time is up, that he is about to be lynched by the enraged men, now takes the ugly-looking Luger (death) and goes sadly to find his friend with the huge and deadly body coupled with the tiny and innocent mind. He finds Lennie sitting hidden in the brush as the sounds of the manhunters come nearer.

> Lennie got up on his knees. "You ain't gonna leave me, are ya, George? I know you ain't."
>
> George came stiffly and sat down beside him. "No."
>
> "I knowed it," Lennie cried. "You ain't that kind."

. . . .

Lennie said, "George."

"Yeah?"

"I done another bad thing."

"It don't make no difference," George said and fell silent again.

Only the topmost ridges were in the sun now. The shadow in the valley [the valley and shadow of death] was blue and soft. From the distance came the sound of men shouting to one another. George turned his head and listened to the shouts.

Lennie said, "George."

"Yeah?"

"Ain't you gonna give me hell?"

"Give you hell?"

"Sure, like you always done before. Like, 'If I didn't have you I'd take my fifty bucks—"

"Jesus Christ, Lennie! You can't remember nothing, but you remember ever' word I say."

. . . .

Lennie looked eagerly at him.

"Go on, George. Ain't you gonna Give me no more hell?"

"No," said George.

The excerpt above indicates Lennie's prayer-like attitude of penitence, confession, deep faith, and the expectation of just punishment. But there is no punishment forthcoming, for George is too heavily saddled with the responsibility of life and death over Lennie—a responsibility of godlike awesomeness constituted of love and so vast that it might stir ancient echoes from the cross on Golgotha, "My God, My God, why has Thou forsaken Me?"

Finally, George can wait no longer. The posse is near. He tells the transported Lennie of the beautiful future, the farm and the rabbits, and the love, where people will give a "hoot in hell" about each other. He assures Lennie that he is not "mad."

He says, "Look down there across the river like you can almost see the place."

Lennie begged, "le's do it now. Le's get that place now."

"Sure, right now. I gotta. We gotta." And George raised the gun and steadied it, and he brought the muzzle of it close to the back of Lennie's head. The hand shook violently, but his face set and his hand steadied. He pulled the trigger. The crash of the shot rolled up the hills and down again. Lennie jarred and then settled slowly forward to the sand, and he lay without quivering. George shivered and looked at the gun; and then he threw it from him, back up on the bank, near the pile of old ashes.

Thus Lennie's perilous journey ends in the merciful hands of his guide and protector, who feels at the moment that this essential deed of love is an act of betrayal. The symbol of death is relegated to the ashheap of the past. And if the reader is impelled to feel that Lennie portrays the Christian figure, he is almost convinced that George, himself, has many of the attributes of the Christ he has been forced to impersonate.

Patterns That Make Meaning

Peter Lisca

Peter Lisca has written extensively on John Steinbeck, including the book *The Wide World of John
Steinbeck*, from which this essay is excerpted. Steinbeck is on record as intending the world of *Of Mice
and Men* to be a microcosm, portraying "the earth
longings of a Lennie who was not to represent
insanity at all but the inarticulate and powerful
yearning of all men." Lisca argues that Steinbeck
succeeds, through the use of language, action, and
symbol as recurring motifs. Recurring actions—for
example, Lennie's repeated destruction of soft
things—create a pattern that the reader expects
will be carried out again. This expectancy of pattern,
Lisca points out, imposes a sense of inevitability and
gives the story meaning.

Concerning [*Of Mice and Men*'s] theme, Steinbeck wrote his
agents, "I'm sorry that you do not find the new book as large
in subject as it should be. I probably did not make my subjects and my symbols clear. The microcosm is rather difficult to handle and apparently I did not get it over—the earth
longings of a Lennie who was not to represent insanity at all
but the inarticulate and powerful yearning of all men. Well,
if it isn't there it isn't there." To Ben Abramson [a Chicago
bookseller who admired Steinbeck's work], he wrote a similar comment on the book's theme: ". . . it's a study of the
dreams and pleasures of everyone in the world."

Such words as "microcosm," "of all men," and "everyone
in the world" indicate that the problem he set himself in *Of
Mice and Men* was similar to that he had solved in his previous novel, *In Dubious Battle*. But whereas in the earlier

Excerpted from *The Wide World of John Steinbeck* by Peter Lisca. Copyright ©1958 by
Rutgers, The State University; copyright ©1986 by Peter Lisca. Reprinted by permission of Rutgers University Press.

work the de-personalized protagonists were easily absorbed into a greater pattern because that pattern was physically present in the novel, in *Of Mice and Men* the protagonists are projected against a very thin background and must suggest or create this larger pattern through their own particularity. To achieve this, Steinbeck makes use of language, action, and symbol as recurring motifs. All three of these motifs are presented in the opening scene, are contrapuntally [with contrasting but parallel elements] developed through the story, and come together again at the end.

A SYMBOLIC PLACE

The first symbol in the novel, and the primary one, is the little spot by the river where the story begins and ends. The book opens with a description of this place by the river, and we first see George and Lennie as they enter this place from the highway to an outside world. It is significant that they prefer spending the night here rather than going on to the bunkhouse at the ranch.

Steinbeck's novels and stories often contain groves, willow thickets by a river, and caves which figure prominently in the action. There are, for example, the grove in *To a God Unknown*, the place by the river in the Junius Maltby story, the two caves and a willow thicket in *The Grapes of Wrath*, the cave under the bridge in *In Dubious Battle*, the caves in *The Wayward Bus*, and the thicket and cave in *The Pearl*. For George and Lennie, as for other Steinbeck heroes, coming to a cave or thicket by the river symbolizes a retreat from the world to a primeval innocence. Sometimes, as in *The Grapes of Wrath*, this retreat has explicit overtones of a return to the womb and rebirth. In the opening scene of *Of Mice and Men* Lennie twice mentions the possibility of hiding out in a cave, and George impresses on him that he must return to this thicket by the river when there is trouble.

While the cave or the river thicket is a "safe place," it is physically impossible to remain there, and this symbol of primeval innocence becomes translated into terms possible in the real world. For George and Lennie it becomes "a little house an' a couple of acres." Out of this translation grows a second symbol, the rabbits, and this symbol serves several purposes. Through synechdoche [a figure of speech in which the part represents the whole] it comes to stand for the "safe place" itself, making a much more easily manipulated symbol than the "house an' a couple of acres." Also, through Lennie's love for the rabbits Steinbeck is able not only to dramatize Lennie's desire for the "safe place," but to define the basis of that desire on a very low level of consciousness—the attraction to soft, warm fur, which is for Lennie the most important aspect of their plans.

LENNIE'S RECURRING ACTION

This transference of symbolic value from the farm to the rabbits is important also because it makes possible the motif of action. This is introduced in the first scene by the dead mouse which Lennie is carrying in his pocket (much as Tom carries the turtle in *The Grapes of Wrath*). As George talks about Lennie's attraction to mice, it becomes evident that the symbolic rabbits will come to the same end—crushed by Lennie's simple, blundering strength. Thus Lennie's killing of mice and later his killing of the puppy set up a pattern which the reader expects to be carried out again. George's story about Lennie and the little girl with the red dress, which he tells twice, contributes to this expectancy of pattern, as do the shooting of Candy's dog, the crushing of Curley's hand, and the frequent appearances of Curley's wife. All these incidents are patterns of the action motif and predict the fate of the rabbits and thus the fate of the dream of a "safe place."

GEORGE'S REPEATED STORY

The third motif, that of language, is also present in the opening scene. Lennie asks George, "Tell me—like you done before," and George's words are obviously in the nature of a ritual. "George's voice became deeper. He repeated his words rhythmically, as though he had said them many times before." The element of ritual is stressed by the fact that even Lennie has heard it often enough to remember its precise language: "*An' live off the fatta the lan'.* . . . An' have *rabbits.* Go on George! Tell about what we're gonna have in the garden and about the rabbits in the cages and about . . ." This ritual is performed often in the story, whenever Lennie feels insecure. And of course it is while Lennie is caught up in this dream vision that George shoots him, so that on one level the vision is accomplished—the dream never interrupted, the rabbits never crushed.

The highly patterned effect achieved by these incremental motifs of symbol, action, and language is the knife edge on which criticism of *Of Mice and Men* divides. For although Steinbeck's success in creating a pattern has been acknowledged, criticism has been divided as to the effect of this achievement. On one side, it is claimed that this strong patterning creates a sense of contrivance and mechanical action, and on the other, that the patterning actually gives a meaningful design to the story, a tone of classic fate. What is obviously needed here is some objective critical tool for determining under what conditions a sense of inevitability (to use a neutral word) should be experienced as mechanical contrivance, and when it should be experienced as catharsis [a release of emotional tension] effected by a sense of fate. Such a tool cannot be forged within the limits of this study; but it is possible to examine the particular circumstances of *Of Mice and Men* more closely before passing judgment.

A BREAK IN THE PATTERN

Although the three motifs of symbol, action, and language build up a strong pattern of inevitability, the movement is not unbroken. About midway in the novel (chapters 3 and 4) there is set up a countermovement which seems to threaten the pattern. Up to this point the dream of "a house an' a couple of acres" seemed impossible of realization. Now it develops that George has an actual farm in mind (ten acres), knows the owners and why they want to sell it: "The ol' people that owns it is flat bust an' the ol' lady needs an operation." He even knows the price—"six hundred dollars." Also, the old workman, Candy, is willing to buy a share in the dream with the three hundred dollars he has saved up. It appears that at the end of the month George and Lennie will have another hundred dollars and that quite possibly they "could swing her for that." In the following chapter this dream and its possibilities are further explored through Lennie's visit with Crooks, the power of the dream manifesting itself in Crooks's conversion from cynicism to optimism. But at the very height of his conversion the mice symbol reappears in the form of Curley's wife, who threatens the dream by bringing with her the harsh realities of the outside world and by arousing Lennie's interest.

The function of Candy's and Crooks's interest and the sudden bringing of the dream within reasonable possibility is to interrupt, momentarily, the pattern of inevitability. But, and this is very important, Steinbeck handles this interruption so that it does not actually reverse the situation. Rather, it insinuates a possibility. Thus, though working against the pattern, this countermovement makes that pattern more credible by creating the necessary ingredient of free will. The story achieves power through a delicate balance of the protagonists' free will and the force of circumstance.

LEVELS OF MEANING

In addition to imposing a sense of inevitability, this strong patterning of events performs the important function of extending the story's range of meanings. This can best be understood by reference to Hemingway's "fourth dimension," which has been defined by [critic] Joseph Warren Beach as an "aesthetic factor" achieved by the protagonists' repeated participation in some traditional "ritual or strategy," and by [critic] Malcolm Cowley as "the almost continual performance of rites and ceremonies" suggesting recurrent patterns of human experience. The incremental motifs of symbol, action, and language which inform *Of Mice and Men* have precisely these effects. The simple story of two migrant workers' dream of a safe retreat, a "clean well-lighted place," becomes itself a pattern or archetype which exists on three levels.

There is the obvious story level on a realistic plane, with its shocking climax. There is also the level of social protest, Steinbeck the reformer crying out against the exploitation of migrant workers. The third level is an allegorical one, its interpretation limited only by the ingenuity of the audience. It could be, as [critic] Carlos Baker suggests, "an allegory of Mind and Body." Using the same kind of dichotomy, the story could also be about the dumb, clumsy, but strong mass of humanity and its shrewd manipulators. This would make the book a more abstract treatment of the two forces of *In Dubious Battle*—the mob and its leaders. The dichotomy could also be that of the unconscious and the conscious, the id and the ego, or any other forces or qualities which have the same structural relationship to each other that do Lennie and George. It is interesting in this connection that the name Leonard means "strong or brave as a lion," and that the name George means "husbandman."

The title itself, however, relates the whole story to still another level which is implicit in the context of [Scottish poet Robert] Burns's poem.

But, Mousie, thou art no thy lane,
In proving foresight may be vain:
The best laid schemes o' mice an' men
    Gang aft a-gley
An' lea'e us nought but grief an' pain
    For promis'd joy.

In the poem, Burns extends the mouse's experience to include that of mankind; in *Of Mice and Men*, Steinbeck extends the experience of two migrant workers to the human condition. "This is the way things are," both writers are saying. On this level, perhaps the most important, Steinbeck is dramatizing the non-teleological [not determined by nature] philosophy which had such a great part in shaping *In Dubious Battle* and which would be fully discussed in *Sea of Cortez*. This level of meaning is indicated by the title originally intended for the book—"Something That Happened." In this light, the ending of the story is, like the ploughman's disrupting of the mouse's nest [in Robert Burns's poem], neither tragic nor brutal, but simply a part of the pattern of events. It is amusing in this regard that a Hollywood director suggested to Steinbeck that someone else kill the girl, so that sympathy could be kept with Lennie.

A DEFINING SUBPLOT

In addition to these meanings which grow out of the book's "pattern," there is what might be termed a subplot which defines George's concern with Lennie. It is easily perceived that George, the "husbandman," is necessary to Lennie; but it has not been pointed out that Lennie is just as necessary to George. Without an explanation of this latter relationship, any allegory posited on the pattern created in *Of Mice and Men* must remain incomplete. Repeatedly, George tells Lennie, "God, you're a lot of trouble. I could get along so easy and so nice if I didn't have you on my tail." But this getting along so easy never means getting a farm of his own. With one important exception, George never mentions the dream except for Lennie's benefit. That his own "dream" is quite different from Lennie's is established early in the novel and often repeated: "God a'mighty, if I was alone I could live so easy. I could go get a job an' work, an' no trouble. No mess at all, and when the end of the month come I could take my fifty bucks and go into town and get whatever I want. Why, I could stay in a cat house all night. I could eat any place I want, hotel or anyplace, and order any damn thing I could think of. An' I could do all that every damn month. Get a gallon whiskey, or set in a pool room and play cards or shoot pool." Lennie has heard this from George so often that in the last scene, when he realizes that he has "done another bad thing," he asks, "Ain't you gonna give me hell? . . . Like, 'If I didn't have you I'd take my fifty bucks—'."

Almost every character in the story asks George why he goes around with Lennie—the foreman, Curley, Slim, and Candy. Crooks, the lonely Negro, doesn't ask George, but he does speculate about it, and shrewdly—"a guy talkin' to another guy and it don't make no difference if he don't hear or understand. The thing is, they're talkin'. . . ." George's explanations vary from outright lies to a simple statement of "We travel together." It is only to Slim, the superior workman with "God-like eyes," that he tells a great part of the truth. Among several reasons, such as his feeling of responsibility for Lennie in return for the latter's unfailing loyalty, and their having grown up together, there is revealed another: "He's dumb as hell, but he ain't crazy. An' I ain't so bright neither, or I wouldn't be buckin' barley for my fifty and found. If I was even a little bit smart, I'd have my own little place, an' I'd be bringin' in my own crops, 'stead of doin' all the work and not getting what comes up outa the ground."

This statement, together with George's repeatedly expressed desire to take his fifty bucks to a cat house and his continual playing of solitaire, reveals that to some extent George needs Lennie as a rationalization for his failure. This is one of the reasons why, after the body of Curley's wife is discovered, George refuses Candy's offer of a partnership which would make the dream a reality and says to him, "I'll work my month an' I'll take my fifty bucks an' I'll stay all night in some lousy cat house. Or I'll set in some poolroom till ever'body goes home. An' then I'll come back an' work another month an' I'll have fifty bucks more." The dream of the farm originates with Lennie and it is only through Lennie, who also makes the dream impossible, that the dream has any meaning for George. An understanding of this dual relationship will do much to mitigate the frequent charge that Steinbeck's depiction of George's attachment is concocted of pure sentimentality. At the end of the novel, George's going off with Slim to "do the town" is more than an escape from grief. It is an ironic and symbolic twist to his dream.

The "real" meaning of the book is neither in the realistic action nor in the levels of allegory. Nor is it in some middle course. Rather, it is in the pattern which informs the story both on the realistic and the allegorical levels, a pattern which Steinbeck took pains to prevent from becoming either trite or mechanical.

But whether because of its realism, its allegory, or its pattern, *Of Mice and Men* was an immediate popular success. It appeared on best-seller lists, was a Book-of-the-Month Club selection, and was sold to Hollywood.

A Game of Cards
as Central Symbol

Michael W. Shurgot

Michael W. Shurgot contributed the following essay
to the *Steinbeck Quarterly*, a literary journal devoted
to the works of John Steinbeck. Shurgot notes that
Steinbeck dots *Of Mice and Men*'s narrative with descriptions of George's games of solitaire, which are
symbolic in three ways. First, Shurgot suggests, the
random arrangement of cards parallels the novel's
world of chance that is beyond man's power to control. Second, the game of solitaire echoes the theme
of isolation. Lastly, solitaire as a game George tries
to win represents his effort—albeit futile—to "win"
his dreams.

Midway through section two of *Of Mice and Men*, after
George and Lennie have met Candy, the boss, and his son
Curley, Steinbeck describes George walking to the table in
the bunkhouse and shuffling some of the playing cards lying
there. Often during the rest of section two and throughout
section three, Steinbeck pictures George playing solitaire
with these cards. Although George's card-playing may seem
just a means of passing time during his and Lennie's first
night on the ranch, the frequency of George's card games
and Steinbeck's careful juxtaposition of them with the
prophetic events of sections two and three indicate that the
game of cards is the central symbol of the entire novel.

SHEER CHANCE

George's card games are generally symbolic in three ways.
Lester Jay Marks writes that Steinbeck's novel is "disciplined
by his non-teleological methods of observing 'phenomena.'
He is concerned not with the *why* but with the *what* and *how*

From Michael Shurgot, "A Game of Cards in Steinbeck's *Of Mice and Men*," *Steinbeck
Quarterly*, vol. 15, nos. 1–2, Winter/Spring 1982. Reprinted by permission of the *Steinbeck Quarterly*. (Notes in the original version have been omitted.)

of the individual's illusions." Steinbeck's original title, "Something That Happened," is, according to Marks, an unsentimental comment upon the "tragic reversal of fortunes" that George and Lennie experience. A non-teleological world is one of chance, of reversals of fortune beyond man's comprehension or his power to control. And a game of cards is an exact symbol of this kind of world. In card games there is no pattern to the cards' random appearance; their sequence is solely a matter of chance. Analogically, although George tries to control Lennie's activities and movements on the ranch, he cannot prevent Lennie's tragic meeting with Curley's wife in the barn.

ISOLATION

Further, George's card game is solitaire. From the opening dialogue between George and Lennie, to the novel's final, terrifying moments, Steinbeck's characters talk about the isolation, rootlessness, and alienation of their lives. Steinbeck introduces the theme of isolation shortly after George and Lennie arrive at the clearing in part one. George laments,

> Guys like us, that work on ranches, are the loneliest guys in the world. They got no family. They don't belong no place. They come to a ranch an' work up a stake and then they go inta town and blow their stake, and the first thing you know they're poundin' their tail on some other ranch. They ain't got nothing to look ahead to.

George's sense of the loneliness and rootlessness of ranchhands is echoed several times in the novel. In section two, Slim observes, "Ain't many guys travel around together. . . . I don't know why. Maybe ever'body in the whole damn world is scared of each other." Early in section three, Slim elaborates on the uniqueness of George's relationship with Lennie:

> Funny how you an' him string along together. . . . I hardly never seen two guys travel together. You know how the hands are, they just come in and get their bunk and work a month, and then they quit and go out alone. Never seem to give a damn about nobody. It jus' seems kinda funny a cuckoo like him and a smart little guy like you travelin' together.

George tells Slim he "ain't got no people," and insists that, although Lennie is a "God damn nuisance most of the time," nonetheless traveling with him is preferable to the loneliness and misery of most ranchhands' lives:

> I seen the guys that go around on the ranches alone. That ain't no good. They don't have no fun. After a long time they

get mean. They get wantin' to fight all the time.

Later, after George has told Candy about his and Lennie's dream of owning their own place, Candy, obviously enthralled at being included in their plans, says that he would leave his share of the place to them "... 'cause I ain't got no relatives nor nothing."

HAND IMAGERY

In his book John Steinbeck: Nature and Myth, *Peter Lisca comments on devices that contribute meaning to* Of Mice and Men, *including Steinbeck's pervasive use of hand imagery.*

On one level [hand imagery] serves simply as an element of characterization. Thus Lennie's hands are more like "paws"; George has "small, strong hands"; Curley keeps one hand in a glove full of vaseline; Crooks has pink palms; Candy is missing a hand; the hands of Curley's wife are referred to only as fingers and red fingernails; Slim has large, capable hands "delicate in their action as those of a temple dancer." But this use of hand imagery falls far short of accounting for the well over one hundred times that it appears in this short novelette. Steinbeck sometimes seems to go out of the way for an excuse to use the word "hand," or insists on using the word when it is already implied, as in "He carried one small willow stick in his hand." Frequently, hands are seen as almost independent of the person himself: "His [Lennie's] hands went into the pocket again"; "Lennie's closed hand slowly obeyed"; "George ... looked at his right hand that had thrown the gun away"; "Slim ... looked down at his hands; he subdued one hand with the other and held it down."

Curiously, the common use of the word "hand" to mean simply a workman, especially on farms and ranches, occurs only once. But perhaps this is the root source of all the hand images. The lives of the characters are so circumscribed that they are more hands than complete men. Curley is said to be "handy," but Lennie "ain't handy." Yet the incident in which Curley attacks Lennie is described entirely in terms of hands; and, symbolically, it concludes with Curley's hands being crushed in the huge paws of Lennie.

On the ranch itself, the most hopelessly alienated characters besides Candy are Crooks and Curley's wife. Crooks, the crippled black stable buck, although serving an important function, is nonetheless isolated in a world of physically powerful white men. Because he is disfigured, and thus less mobile than the ranchhands, he is ironically more permanent than they, but he is barred from their quarters and sleeps in a "long box filled with straw," a symbolic coffin. Echoing George's remarks about the psychological effects of constant loneliness, Crooks complains bitterly to Lennie, "A guy goes nuts if he ain't got nobody. Don't make no difference who the guy is, long's he's with you. . . . I tell ya a guy gets too lonely an' he gets sick." Curley's wife is equally lonely, frustrated, and alienated. She hates staying in the "two-by-four house" with Curley, who "spends all his time sayin' what he's gonna do to guys he don't like, and he don't like nobody." She insists that at one time she "could of went with shows," and that "a guy tol' me he could put me in pictures." But instead, she now spends Saturday nights 'talkin' to a bunch of bindle stiffs—a nigger an' a dumdum and a lousy ol' sheep—an' likin' it because they ain't nobody else." Although the circumstances of their lives on the ranch are quite different, Crooks and Curley's wife are similarly isolated within and segregated from the white, predominantly masculine world of the novel. Fortune has been kind to neither Crooks nor Curley's wife, and their lives emphasize the pervasive isolation (and occasionally despair) that haunts Steinbeck's characters.

GEORGE'S EFFORTS TO "WIN"

Besides symbolizing the lonely, disjointed lives of the ranchhands and the alienation of Crooks and Curley's wife, George's games of solitaire are symbolic in a third way. George tries, quite naturally, to "win" his games of solitaire, and when considered along with several of his remarks to Lennie, such efforts at victory become quite ironic. Early in section one, after pleading with Lennie not to "do no bad things like you done in Weed," George describes, as he does frequently in the novel, what he could do if he were alone:

> "God, you're a lot of trouble," said George. "I could get along so easy and so nice if I didn't have you on my tail. I could live so easy and maybe have a girl."

Twice more in part one, George repeats this sentiment. The first time, Lennie's innocent wish for some ketchup precipitates one of George's most violent explosions against him in the novel. George angrily recounts their narrow escape from Weed—"You crazy son-of-a-bitch. You keep me in hot water all the time"—and brutally claims, "I wisht I could put you in a cage with about a million mice an' let you have fun." Moments later, after Lennie pathetically insists that had they any ketchup George could have all of it, George says, "When I think of the swell time I could have without you, I go nuts. I never get no peace." Just after returning to the clearing in part six, Lennie says, "George gonna wish he was alone an' not have me botherin' him." Shortly after Lennie's remark, George is alone, and as lonely as the other ranchhands he describes earlier in part one. Although he certainly wants and needs Lennie to fulfill their dream together, George's frequent wish to be alone, to be free of the burden of minding Lennie, is ironically forecast in his frequent resorts to solitaire in the first half of the novel.

INTERWEAVING OF CARD SYMBOLISM

Steinbeck enhances the general symbolism of George's games of solitaire by carefully interweaving them into the narrative of sections two and three. George first plays with the cards during his conversation with Candy about Curley and his wife. Candy explains that Curley is a fighter and has become "cockier'n ever since he got married." George remarks that Curley had better "watch out for Lennie," walks to the table and picks up the cards, and fumbles with them continually as Candy describes Curley's "glove . . . fulla vaseline" and his wife:

> "Wait'll you see Curley's wife."
> George cut the cards again and put out a solitaire lay, slowly and deliberately. "Purty?" he asked casually.

Steinbeck's careful positioning of Candy's description of Curley's wife and George's first hand of solitaire juxtaposes the immediate cause of the failure of George and Lennie's dream and the ultimate consequence of that failure for George: his solitude. A similar juxtaposition occurs moments later. Candy says to George, "Well, you look her over, mister. You see if she ain't a tart." Steinbeck writes:

> George laid down his cards thoughtfully, turned his piles of three. He built four clubs on his ace pile. . . . George stared at his solitaire lay, and then he flounced the cards together and turned around to Lennie.

George warns Lennie about Curley, whom he correctly perceives as a threat to their plans, and repeats his instructions to him about returning to the pool in the river should trouble occur. Curley's wife enters immediately, and Lennie's twice-repeated "She's purty" elicits George's fierce warning to him about her being "jail bait" and his insistence that he and Lennie must stay at the ranch until they make their stake:

> "We gotta keep it till we get a stake. We can't help it, Lennie. We'll get out jus' as soon as we can. I don't like it no better than you do." He went back to the table and set out a new solitaire hand.

George's card games precede and follow the appearance of Curley's wife and Lennie's reactions to her, thus symbolically framing their first meeting in a realm of chance. Further, when Slim enters he sits down at the table across from George. While Slim plays with the cards, he talks to Carlson about his dog's pups and Candy's old dog. This conversation foreshadows Lennie's death; and the sense of his and the dog's similar fates is suggested by the hand of cards that George and Slim, with ironic nonchalance, manipulate during this scene. Section two closes with George's return to the cards amid his promise to Lennie to ask Slim about a pup, thus initiating the chain of events that leads to Lennie's presence in the barn when Curley's wife tempts him the following Sunday.

Section three opens with George's confiding in Slim about Lennie's troubles in Weed. Twice during their dialogue Steinbeck describes George playing solitaire:

> "'Course he ain't mean. But he gets in trouble alla time because he's so God damn dumb. Like what happened in Weed—." He stopped, stopped in the middle of turning over a card.

And

> Slim's eyes were level and unwinking. He nodded very slowly. "So what happens?"
>
> George carefully built his line of solitaire cards.

Steinbeck's careful interweaving of George's hand of solitaire with his narrative of Lennie's seizure of the girl in Weed is his most effective apposition in the novel. Lennie's actions in Weed clearly presage his killing Curley's wife, and George will be alone after he shoots Lennie.

Steinbeck employs this card symbolism variously in the rest of section three. Just before Carlson shoots Candy's dog, George and Whit start a game of euchre, but when Whit mentions Curley's wife, he drops his cards and George immediately lays out another hand of solitaire. After Carlson and Lennie return to the bunkhouse and Curley inquires about his wife and Slim, Lennie joins George at the table:

> He got up from his bunk and sat down at the table, across
> from George. Almost automatically George shuffled the cards
> and laid out his solitaire hand. He used a deliberate, thought-
> ful, [sic] slowness.

George's "automatically" laying out his solitaire hand as he
sits across from Lennie is acutely ironic and prophetic, for
George will be as solitary as the rest of the ranchhands after
Lennie's death. A moment later, as George "look[s] carefully
at the solitaire hand," he mentions that Andy Cushman is "in
San Quentin right now on account of a tart." As an anony-
mous tart was responsible for Andy Cushman's fate, so Curley's wife, whom Candy describes as a "tart" in section two,
will be responsible for Lennie's. Even as he and Lennie talk,
George's conversation obliquely foreshadows the novel's cli-
mactic scene and ironically reinforces the symbolism of his
game of solitaire.

SHATTERED ILLUSIONS

Lennie's repetitive questioning about their "little place"
abruptly changes the mood in the bunkhouse. "George's
hands stopped working with the cards. His voice was growing warmer." Significantly, George abandons the cards
while describing their dream, as if its fulfillment were
within their own control, beyond chance. Indeed, Candy's
unexpected offer of his $300 suddenly convinces George that
his and Lennie's long quest may finally be successful. "They
all sat still, all bemused by the beauty of the thing, each
mind was popped into the future when this lovely thing
should come about." But their illusion is quickly shattered.
It is sheer chance, like the unexpected appearance of a card,
and brutal irony that Lennie is still smiling "with delight at
the memory of the ranch" when the enraged Curley, after
being repulsed by Slim, enters the bunkhouse spoiling for a
fight and misinterprets Lennie's smile. In the ensuing battle
between Lennie and Curley, Steinbeck vividly and prophet-
ically describes the terrible strength that will destroy the
dream and insulate George: "The next minute Curley was
flopping like a fish on a line, and his closed fist was lost in
Lennie's big hand." Steinbeck uses the same image to describe the death of Curley's wife: "'Don't you go yellin',' he
said, and he shook her; and her body flopped like a fish."

In the final moments of section three, Steinbeck's disciplined non-teleological vision is clearly evident; chance rules in the bunkhouse as later it will in the barn. The genius of Steinbeck's narrative in *Of Mice and Men* lies in the consistency of this vision, and in George's card games Steinbeck provides an exact symbol of the unpredictable, often merciless world in which his characters vainly strive to maintain their dignity and fulfill their dreams.

Ed Ricketts's Influence on Steinbeck's Fiction

Richard Astro

For eighteen years Steinbeck enjoyed an unusually close friendship with marine biologist Ed Ricketts. According to some critics, the serious reader of Steinbeck must understand Ricketts's scientific worldview because it is strongly reflected in Steinbeck's fiction. Richard Astro, author of *John Steinbeck and Edward F. Ricketts: The Shaping of a Novelist*, comments on how and to what extent Ricketts's nonteleological thinking—an approach that records what happens without explaining why—influenced the creation of *Of Mice and Men*. Astro cautions the reader against reading *Of Mice and Men* strictly as a nonteleological tale. Rather, he argues, Steinbeck used the approach as a fictional method, as a means of recording data.

It is possible to read the grim events in *Of Mice and Men* either as tragedy or as dark comedy (the "triumph of the indomitable will [George's] to survive [cited in Warren French's *John Steinbeck*]"). Both approaches contain a substantial degree of truth, but one must not allow either to obscure Steinbeck's uniquely delicate handling of his fictional materials, which accounts for the book's particular excellence. For Steinbeck neither blames nor accuses in *Of Mice and Men;* he simply tells a story about the way in which "the best laid schemes o' mice an' men gang aft a'gley." The original title of the novelette was "Something That Happened," and while one can read it as simple tragedy, as social protest (against the mistreatment of rootless and helpless farm workers), or on a symbolic level in which the characters can be extended to any symbolic dimension, *Of Mice and Men* is simultaneously a non-teleological tale which simply says,

Excerpted from *John Steinbeck and Edward F. Ricketts: The Shaping of a Novelist* by Richard Astro. Copyright ©1973 by the University of Minnesota. Reprinted by permission of the University of Minnesota Press.

"This is what happened." Viewed this way, "Steinbeck's achievement in *Of Mice and Men* is even more impressive: the hardest task a writer can set himself is to tell the story of 'something that happened' without explaining 'why'—and make it convincing and moving" [cited in Antonia Seixas's "John Steinbeck and the Non-Teleological Bus," in *What's Doing on the Monterey Peninsula*, March 1947].

ANIMAL INSTINCTS

In a pioneering essay written in 1941, Edmund Wilson notes Steinbeck's preoccupation with biology and his tendency to animalize human beings.

The chief subject of Mr. Steinbeck's fiction has been not those aspects of humanity in which it is most thoughtful, imaginative, constructive, nor even those aspects of animals that seem most attractive to humans, but rather the processes of life itself. In the natural course of nature, living organisms are continually being destroyed, and among the principal things that destroy them are the predatory appetite and the competitive instinct that are necessary for the very survival of eating and breeding creatures. This impulse of the killer has been preserved in a simpleton like Lennie in a form in which it is almost innocent; and yet Lennie has learned from his more highly developed friend that to yield to it is to do something "bad." In his struggle against the instinct, he loses. Is Lennie bad or good? He is betrayed as, Mr. Steinbeck implies, all our human intentions are: by the uncertainties of our animal nature.

With regard to the impact of Ricketts' thinking on Steinbeck's fiction, it would be very convenient if we could say that *Of Mice and Men* is a fictionalized version of Ricketts' doctrine of non-teleological thinking, and that Steinbeck shows he is not concerned with what "could be" or "should be" but only with what "is." But to do so would be to deny the novelist's insistence on the importance of man's voluntary acceptance of his responsibilities, which is based on his belief that man owes something to man. Viewed in perspective, what Steinbeck seems to be doing in *Of Mice and Men* is using Ricketts' ideas about non-teleological thinking not as theme, but as fictional method. He tells the story of Lennie and George from a nonblaming point of view, but never does he suggest the unimportance of the teleological considerations symbolized by Lennie's dream.

Actually, Steinbeck's method in *Of Mice and Men* emerges through the consciousness of Slim, the jerkline skinner and "prince of the ranch," who moves "with a majesty only achieved by royalty and master craftsmen." It is Slim, a character whose "ear heard more than was said to him" and whose "slow speech had overtones not of thought, but of understanding beyond thought," who understands George and Lennie's land hunger but who also knows that the dream must fail. And it is Slim who affirms the need for direct, purposive action by George after Lennie kills Curley's wife. "You hadda George. I swear you hadda."

Significantly, Ricketts observed in one section of his essay on non-teleological thinking that the term *non-teleological* encompassed more than thinking: "*Modus operandi* might be better—a method of handling data of any sort." Indeed, says Ricketts, "the value of it [non-teleological thinking] as a tool in increased understanding cannot be denied." This is the one aspect of Ricketts' notion that particularly appealed to Steinbeck; the use of the non-teleological approach as a means of handling the data of fiction. And Steinbeck is generally at his best when he writes in this manner; when, in such works as *In Dubious Battle*, "Johnny Bear," "The Snake," and "The Leader of the People," but most particularly in *Of Mice and Men*, he achieves what T.K. Whipple calls "the middle distance" in which he places his characters "not too close nor too far away" so that "we can see their performances with greatest clarity and fullness."

As an undergraduate at Stanford, Steinbeck learned from his creative writing teacher, Edith Ronald Mirrielees, that the storywriter's "medium is the spot light, not the search light." And it is the spotlight which illumines the characters and events in *Of Mice and Men*. Unlike *To a God Unknown*, in which Steinbeck's tendency to philosophize seriously mars what is otherwise a highly important piece of writing, the novelist's use of Ricketts' *modus operandi* in *Of Mice and Men* enabled him to avoid pretentious philosophizing while recording his beliefs. And in telling his story about the fractured dreams of mice and men with a precision and lucidity unexcelled in any of his other works, Steinbeck testifies to the fact that Ed Ricketts not only helped teach him how to "live into life," but that he also had a hand in helping him record his observations of it.

CHAPTER 3

A Critical Selection

READINGS ON
OF MICE AND MEN

Lyricism in
Of Mice and Men

R. Ganapathy

R. Ganapathy contributed this essay to the *Literary Criterion*, published in India, for a special 1962 edition on American literature. Ganapathy contends that Steinbeck is unrivaled in his ability to find poetic beauty in ordinary, unsophisticated life. In Steinbeck's hands, rustic characters take on noble qualities and the rural setting becomes a nostalgic, pastoral fantasy. Steinbeck achieves this lyrical effect, according to Ganapathy, through theme, characterization, and narrative.

A striking and characteristic quality in much of what Steinbeck writes, is lyricism, and particularly in his novelette, 'Of Mice and Men' this lyrical strain is manifest in theme, characterization and narrative. . . .

Steinbeck delineates George and Lennie with a poetic tenderness and sympathy that is typical of him. George is an intelligent and hard working young man, but highly impractical and imaginative, while his friend and associate, Lennie, is a half-wit, who always needs the help and protection of George. Primitive as they are, there is yet a poetic beauty in their affectionate relationship to each other. There is a mutual trust in their fundamental goodness and warmth of friendship, and there are re-iterative references in the novel to each other's natural nobility.

The sheer animal strength of Lennie always destines him to fatal consequences and it also brings George endless trouble and worry. But it is amazing how they stick to each other, despite many adverse happenings.

Thus, Steinbeck's 'Of Mice and Men' is a lyrical story and study of two noble savages of Salinas Valley in California, and of their heart-aching hunger for a bit of land.

Excerpted from R. Ganapathy, "Steinbeck's *Of Mice and Men*: A Study of Lyricism Through Primitivism," *Literary Criterion*, vol. 5, no. 3, Winter 1962. Reprinted by permission.

NOSTALGIA FOR THE PRIMITIVE

This pervasive lyricism in the novel comes out of Steinbeck's loyalty to rural California. What must have been a cold, journalistic documentation of rustic life in Salinas Valley, becomes in the hands of Steinbeck, a fine pastoral phantasy in which there is the novelist's romantic assertion of faith in the beauty of ordinary, unsophisticated life. Rural life may be elemental, primitive and even awkward, but it has its own enchantment and poetry. He is at once in emotional sympathy with the lives of these rustics and he portrays them with an understanding, frankness and awareness that are rare among other contemporary American writers. He 'sings' in modern American prose that becomes racy and poetic in his hands, of the primitive rustics' joys and sorrows, their hopes and aspirations, their fears, failures and their daily tragedies. The nostalgia for the primitive impels him to write emotionally, movingly. It will be interesting to consider Steinbeck as a writer of ballads in prose, of Californian folk life. Other American men of letters like Henry Miller and Robinson Jeffers have 'used' California in their works, but in bringing out the essential poetry of natural, primitive life, Steinbeck is unique and unrivalled.

In so many ways, Steinbeck, in this novel and in several others like *The Grapes of Wrath, The Red Pony,* and *Tortilla Flat,* seems to do what Wordsworth did in nineteenth century romantic poetry. We may look upon Steinbeck's works as unconscious exemplification in prose of Wordsworth's idea of poetry which he enunciated in his Preface to the *Lyrical Ballads.* If to Wordsworth the meanest flower did seem beautiful, to Steinbeck the humblest rustic does look and speak as a poet does.

Steinbeck's studied handling of colloquial prose rhythms heightens the lyrical effect which he achieves by repetition. Certain powerfully racy and colloquial words and sentences, profane and shocking at times, are so artistically repeated over and over again that they sink into the reader's mind as refrains in a song. Such examples in 'Of Mice and Men' are: 'I like beans with ketchup', 'An' live off the fatta the lan', 'An' have rabbits', 'This ain't no good place. I wanna get outa here', 'He ain't mean', and 'I done another bad thing'. In 'The Grapes of Wrath', the oft repeated swear words, 'Them goddam Oakies' attain a poetic significance, and the emotive value of these words reveal Steinbeck's own attitude to the suffering, migratory people of Oklahoma. He thus exploits these refrains by orchestrating them like a composer, at the most suitable places and the effect he thus achieves is highly poetic and dramatic.

MOOD PROSE

To this he adds another favourite technique of his. What are these Californian folks after all, without the essential, elemental background of nature and landscape? So Steinbeck describes these in a prose that is highly charged with imagery and poetry, and in so doing, establishes the primary relationship between natural forces and primitive man. In fact no other American poet, dramatist or novelist has described the California landscape so effectively and evocatively as Steinbeck has done. In this contrapuntal [with contrasting but parallel elements] interplay between rural naturalism and rustic realism, Steinbeck wields a prose that may be termed 'mood prose', which, like mood music, describes the setting and dictates the atmosphere, as for instance in these sentences: 'The day was going fast now. Only the tops of the Gabilan mountains flamed with the light of the sun that had gone from the valley. A water snake slipped along on the pool, its head held up like a little periscope. The reeds jerked slightly in the current. Far off toward the high-way a man shouted something, and another man shouted back. The sycamore limbs rustled under a little wind that died immediately'.

In poetizing the rustics in their naturalistic background, Steinbeck compares closely with Thomas Hardy, but there is a difference. The impact of modern science upon agricultural England was a human predicament for Hardy, which left him pessimistic, while the urbanization of rural America is a challenge which incites Steinbeck to protest indignantly against social exploitation and economic injustice, particularly in his great work, *The Grapes of Wrath.*

Steinbeck has always a flair for comic situations. The farm labourers at Curley's ranch do not fail to notice even the smallest thing that contributes to the comedy of life. Curley's wife ever in search of her husband, young Curley getting his 'han' 'caught' in a 'machine', and Whit's account of old Susy's brothel are a few examples of Steinbeck's description of the rural comedy which relieves the profound, tragic atmosphere of the novel. Steinbeck in this respect goes hand in hand with the other regionalist-naturalist, Erskine Caldwell. Both of them have a partiality for describing in realistic terms the rugged banter and folk ribaldry of the rustics. Caldwell's Ty Ty in *God's Little Acre* and Steinbeck's Grand Pa Joad in *The Grapes of Wrath* are indeed two famous hard-swearing, deep-drinking fictional twins in contemporary American literature.

Lennie's animalism is a natal flaw [present from birth] that brings about his final catastrophe. His inordinate desire to pet mice and rabbits, and his killing them while petting, lead him on to do the same with Curley's wife, whom he kills as he would a mouse. There is a fatality in his very touch and the mouse itself becomes a symbol of death.

And finally when George shoots him through the head, while lulling him with stories of the farm that they will never buy and own, it is very difficult for the readers to reconcile themselves to this gruesome end. Our sympathies are already with Lennie, however bad and primitive he might be, and his death comes as a shock to us. Steinbeck does make us think here of the inexplicableness of life.

Thus, 'Of Mice and Men' is a consciously created classical tragedy in which the figures, though sparsely drawn, invite a close comparison with the great figures in Greek tragedy, by virtue of their naturally fatal flaws.

The modern Indian, with his age-old background of rural life and with his peculiar advantage of orientation in the best ideals of the East and the West, is perhaps more fortunately situated to receive Steinbeck than the Americans themselves.

There is a close affinity between the traditional Indian life and the life that Steinbeck portrays in his comic and serious lyric novels, and because of this perhaps, his impact on Indian writers of fiction, with reference to thematics and technique, has been very profound and significant.

A Mechanical Story with Subhuman Characters

Mark Van Doren

As literary editor for the *Nation*, Mark Van Doren
panned *Of Mice and Men* shortly after its publication in 1937. His review calls the novel predictable
and mechanical. He claims the characters are so
subhuman as to be wholly unrealistic: All the characters except for Slim are blatantly evil, dangerous,
or ignorant. Van Doren adds that Slim's godlike
qualities leave him as hopelessly above the range
of normal human behavior as the rest of the characters are below it.

All but one of the persons in Mr. Steinbeck's extremely brief
novel are subhuman if the range of the word human is understood to coincide with the range thus far established by
fiction. Two of them are evil, one of them is dangerous without meaning to be, and all of them are ignorant; all of them,
that is, except the one who shall be named hereafter. Far
from knowing the grammar of conduct, they do not even
know its orthography [most basic building blocks, its "letters
and words"]. No two of their thoughts are consecutive, nor
for that matter do they think; it is rather that each of them
follows some instinct as a bull follows the chain which runs
through a hole in his nose, or as a crab moves toward its
prey. The scene is a ranch in California, and the bunk-house
talk is terrific: God damn, Jesus Christ, what the hell, you
crazy bastard, I gotta gut ache, and things like that. The dialect never varies, just as the story never runs uphill.

George and Lennie, the itinerant workers who come to the
ranch one day with a dream of the little farm they will own as
soon as they get the jack [slang for money] together, seem to
think their new job will last at least that long; but the reader

From *"Of Mice and Men* by John Steinbeck," review by Mark Van Doren, from the
March 6, 1937, issue of the *Nation.* Reprinted with permission of the *Nation.*

knows from the beginning that it will not last, for Lennie is a half-witted giant with a passion for petting mice—or rabbits, or pups, or girls—and for killing them when they don't like it. He is doomed in this book to kill Curley's wife; that is obvious; and then—Lennie, you see, cannot help shaking small helpless creatures until their necks are broken, just as George cannot relinquish his dream, and just as Curley cannot ever stop being a beast of jealousy. They are wound up to act that way, and the best they can do is run down; which is what happens when Mr. Steinbeck comes to his last mechanical page.

What, however, of the one exception? Ah, he is Slim the jerkline skinner, the tall man with the "God-like eyes" that get fastened on you so that you can't think of anything else for a while. "There was a gravity in his manner and a quiet so profound that all talk stopped when he spoke.... His hatchet face was ageless. He might have been thirty-five or fifty. His ear heard more than was said to him, and his slow speech had overtones not of thought, but of understanding beyond thought. His hands, large and lean, were as delicate in their action as those of a temple dancer." He looks through people and beyond them: a feat never accomplished save in mechanical novels. And he understands—why, he understands everything that Mr. Steinbeck understands. It is the merest accident of education that he talks like the rest; "Jesus, he's jes' like a kid, ain't he," he says. If he had his creator's refinement of tongue he could write such sentences as this one which introduces Lennie: "His arms did not swing at his sides, but hung loosely and only moved because the heavy hands were pendula." It wouldn't have done to write pendulums. That would have given the real sound and look of Lennie, and besides it is a real word.

Mr. Steinbeck, I take it, has not been interested in reality of any kind. His jerkline skinner (mule driver) is as hopelessly above the human range as Lennie or Candy or Curley's painted wife is below it. All is extreme here; everybody is a doll; and if there is a kick in the story it is given us from some source which we cannot see, as when a goose walks over our grave, or as when in the middle of the night the telephone rings sharply and it is the wrong number. We shall remember it about that long.

Gender in
Of Mice and Men

Mark Spilka

Mark Spilka examines three characters in his
analysis of gender in *Of Mice and Men*. According to
Spilka, Curley's wife represents aggressive sexuality
and the exploitation of men's lust. While George
retreats from this sexual trap, the infantile Lennie
remains at the mercy of his destructive sexual
impulses, which move him to violence. Spilka adds
that Steinbeck may be portraying his own hostility
toward adult sexuality through his portrayal of these
characters.

> Nearly everyone in the world has appetites and impulses,
> trigger emotions, islands of selfishness, lusts just beneath the
> surface. And most people either hold such things in check or
> indulge them secretly. Cathy knew not only these impulses in
> others but how to use them for her own gain. It is quite pos-
> sible that she did not believe in any other tendencies in
> humans, for while she was preternaturally alert in some di-
> rections she was completely blind in others. Cathy learned
> when she was very young that sexuality with all its attendant
> yearnings and pains, jealousies and taboos, is the most dis-
> turbing impulse humans have.

My epigraph is from Steinbeck's postwar novel *East of Eden*,
published in 1952. It concerns a woman called Cathy Ames
who deserts her husband and newborn twins to become the
successful proprietor of a California whorehouse. In his di-
aries for the composition of the novel Steinbeck calls this
woman a "monster" and says he will prove to his readers
that such monsters actually exist. His choice of her as the ar-
chetypal mother of a California family, his peculiarly Miltonic view of her as an exploiter of men's lusts, and his
awareness of the exploitability of such feelings—this complex of psychological tendencies in the later Steinbeck has
much to do, I think, with the force behind his early social

Excerpted from Mark Spilka, "Of George and Lennie and Curley's Wife: Sweet Violence
in Steinbeck's Eden," *Modern Fiction Studies*, vol. 20 (1974). Copyright 1974, The Johns
Hopkins University Press. Reprinted by permission of the publishers.

fiction. I want to examine one of his early social tales, *Of Mice and Men,* with that possibility in mind. . . .

NATURAL FREEDOM

The sycamore grove by the Salinas River, so lovingly described in the opening lines, is more than scene setting: it is an attempt to evoke the sense of freedom in nature which, for a moment only, the protagonists will enjoy. By a path worn hard by boys and hobos two migrant laborers appear. The first man is mouselike: "small and quick, dark of face, with restless eyes and sharp, strong features. Every part of him was defined: small, strong hands, slender arms, a thin and bony nose." He is the planner from the poem by Robert Burns: as with other mice and men, his best arrangements will often go astray. A bus driver has just tricked him and his friend into getting out four miles from the ranch where jobs await them. Now he decides to stay in the small grove near the river because he "like[s] it here." There will be work tomorrow, but tonight he can "lay right here and look up" at the sky through sycamore leaves; he can dream and plan with his friend of the farm they will never own.

The nearest town is Soledad, which means "lonely place" in Spanish; the town where they last worked, digging a cesspool, was Weed. Their friendship is thus quickly placed as a creative defense against rank loneliness; it will be reinforced, thematically, by the hostility and guardedness of bunkhouse life, and by the apparent advance of their dream toward realization. But the secluded grove, the site of natural freedom, provides the only substantiation their dream will ever receive; and when our mouselike planner tells his friend to return there in case of trouble, we sense that the dream will end where it essentially begins, in this substantiating site.

The second man to appear is "opposite" to the first: "a huge man, shapeless of face, with large, pale eyes, with wide, sloping shoulders" and loose-hanging arms; he walks heavily, "dragging his feet a little, the way a bear drags his paws." This bearlike man becomes equine when they reach the grove: flinging himself down, he drinks from the pool there, "snorting into the water like a horse." Then again like a bear, he dips his whole head under, "hat and all," sits up so the hat drips down his back, and "dabble[s] his big paw in the water."

These animal actions and his childish speech place him for us quickly as an idiot. What the first man plans for, the second already has. Like other Steinbeck idiots—Tularecito in *The Pastures of Heaven* (1932), Johnny Bear in *The Long Valley* (1938)—he participates in natural life freely, has access to its powers, and his attraction for Steinbeck is his freedom to use those powers without blame or censure. More nearly animal than human, more nearly child than man, he eludes responsibility for his actions. Again like the natural artist Tularecito and the uncanny mimic Johnny Bear, he is extraordinarily gifted; he has superhuman strength which inevitably threatens a society whose rules he cannot comprehend. He is thus the perfect denizen of the secluded grove where, for a moment, natural freedom reigns; the perfect victim, too, for an intruding social world which will eventually deny that freedom.

In his pocket the idiot carries an actual mouse, dead from too much handling. Later he kills a puppy with playful buffeting. A child fondling "lesser" creatures, he is Steinbeck's example of senseless killing in nature. He is also part of an ascending hierarchy of power. His name is Lennie *Small*, by which Steinbeck means subhuman, animal, childlike, without power to judge or master social fate. His friend's name, George Milton, puts him by literary allusion near the godhead, above subhuman creatures, able to judge whether they should live or die. The title and epilogue of *In Dubious Battle* (1936) were also drawn from Milton, whose grand judgmental abstractions take humble proletarian forms in Steinbeck's world. Thus, in a later set-up scene . . . , old Candy, the lowly bunkhouse sweeper, says that he should have shot his own decrepit dog—should not have let a stranger do it for him. George too will decide that he must shoot Lennie, like a mad rather than a decrepit dog, for the unplanned murder of another man's wife; that he cannot allow strangers to destroy him.

THE DECISION TO KILL LENNIE

Both shootings have been sanctioned by the jerkline skinner, Slim, "prince of the ranch," who moves "with a majesty achieved only by royalty" and looks with "calm, God-like eyes" upon his bunkhouse world. Since his word is "law" for the migrant farmhands, and since Milton, a rational farmhand, can recognize and accept such godlike laws, he must choose to shoot his friend. By *East of Eden* Steinbeck would conclude that it is choice which separates men from animals, a belief which supports one critic's view of George's decision as "mature." But it is not his "ordinariness" which George will accept in destroying Lennie and the comforting dream they share, as this critic holds: it is his *humanness*, his responsibility for actions which the animal Lennie, for all his vital strength, cannot comprehend.

And yet George will be diminished—made "ordinary"—by his choice. As many critics insist, he uses Lennie selfishly, draws from him a sense of power, of superiority, which he sorely needs. If he is sensitive to Lennie's feelings—cares for and about him in demonstrable ways—he also "lords" it over him almost vengefully. The opening scene indicates nicely how much petty satisfaction he takes in giving Lennie orders and complaining about the burden of thinking for him. But more than this: the scene creates a causal expectation—that one way or another Lennie will always feed this satisfaction, will always do, in effect, what George desires—which means that George himself invites the troubles ahead, makes things go astray, uses Lennie to provoke and settle his own quarrel with a hostile world.

This is evident enough when he tells Lennie not to talk, to leave job negotiations to him so as not to expose his idiocy before his strength has been displayed. Inevitably bosses are annoyed when Lennie fails to speak for himself; suspicions are aroused, and future troubles more or less ensured. This is exactly what George desires, first with the boss of the Soledad ranch, then with two extensions of the boss's power—his son Curley and Curley's straying wife. George resents these people so much, and pins such frightening taboos on them, that Lennie is bound to panic when he meets them, to clutch with his tremendous strength—like a child caught with some forbidden object—and so punish people whom George openly dislikes. In a very real sense, then, George lordfully creates the troubles for which Lennie will himself be blamed and punished—though he only obeys his master's vengeful voice.

ECHOES OF THE ARTHURIAN CIRCLE

This is to move from social into psychological conflict: but Steinbeck, in taking a boss's son and his wife as sources of privileged pressure on migrant farmhands, has moved there before us. He has chosen aggressive sexuality as the force, in migrant life, which undermines the friendship dream. This variation on the Garden of Eden theme is, to say the least, peculiar. There is something painfully adolescent about the notion of a cooperative farm run by bachelor George and idiot Lennie, with the probable help of a maimed old man and a defiant black cripple. The grouping is not unlike the Arthurian circle around Danny in *Tortilla Flat* (1935): four good-hearted lads sticking together against the world, who can drop work and go into town whenever they want to see "a carnival or a circus ... or a ball game." Their self-employment seems more like freedom from adult supervision than from harsh conditions; and their friendship seems more like an escape from the coarseness of adult sexuality than from bunkhouse loneliness. Even their knightly pledge to help each other seems oddly youthful. That Steinbeck read the Arthurian legends at an early age, and that he also worked on ranches during boyhood summers, may be relevant here: for the world of friendship he imagines is a boy's world, a retreat from the masculine grossness and insecurity of the bunkhouse, from whorehouse visits and combative marriages like Curley's, which in his youth he must have found disturbing. George Milton shows enough insecurity and disgust about sex, and enough hostility toward women to make these speculations about Steinbeck's choices worth pursuing. . . .

Lennie first pets Curley's wife, then breaks her neck without any awareness that she provokes both reactions. His conscious desires are simple: to stroke something furry, and to stop the furry thing from yelling so George won't be mad at him. But George had predicted this episode, has called Curley's wife a rattrap, a bitch, a piece of jailbait; and he has roundly expressed disgust at Curley's glove full of Vaseline, which softens the hand that strokes his wife's genitals. Lennie has obligingly crushed that hand for George, and now he obligingly breaks the rattrap for him, that snare for mice and men which catches both in its furry toils.

In the play Steinbeck goes out of his way to make it clear that George's hostility to Curley's wife prefigures Lennie's. In a scene not in the novel, he arranges an exchange in the Negro Crooks's room in which George's arm is raised in anger against this woman: he is about to strike her for threatening the friendship dream, for trying to "mess up what we're gonna do." Then Curley's father arrives, the girl retreats from the room, and George lowers his hand as the scene closes.

STEINBECK'S HOSTILITY TOWARD WOMEN

As such manipulations imply, Steinbeck projects his own hostilities through George and Lennie. He has himself given this woman no other name but "Curley's wife" as if she had no personal identity for him. He has presented her, in the novel, as vain, provocative, vicious (she threatens Crooks with lynching, for instance, when he tries to defy her), and only incidentally lonely. Now in the play—perhaps in response to the criticisms of friends—he reverses her portrait. She is no longer vicious (her lynching threat has been written out of the script), and she is not even provocative: she is just a lonely woman whose attempts at friendliness are misunderstood. Thus she makes her first entrance with a line transferred from a later scene in the novel: "I'm just lookin' for somebody to talk to," she says, in case we might think otherwise. . . .

Steinbeck's sentimentality is the obverse side of his hostility. We see this in the novel when it breaks through in another form, as a mystic moment of redemption for Curley's wife. Thus, as she lies dead in the barn "the meanness and the plannings and the discontent and the ache for attention" disappear from her face; she becomes sweet and young, and her rouged cheeks and reddened lips make her seem alive and sleeping lightly "under a half-covering of hay." At which point sound and movement stop, and, "as sometimes happens," a moment settles and hovers and remains "for much, much more than a moment." Then time wakens and moves sluggishly on. Horses stamp in the barn, their halter chains clink, and outside, men's voices become "louder and clearer."

Restored to natural innocence through death, Curley's wife is connected—for a timeless moment—with the farm dream. Then men's voices and stamping horses indicate the sexual restlessness she provokes in adult life. Only when sexually quiescent—as in death or childhood—can she win this author's heart.

Interestingly, Steinbeck shares this predilection with William Faulkner, whose idiot Benjy in *The Sound and the Fury* (1929) wants his sister Caddie to smell like trees and is troubled when perfume or sexual odors suffuse that smell. Benjy is gelded, not shot, when he later innocently

JOHN STEINBECK ON CURLEY'S WIFE

Actress Claire Luce played Curley's wife in the Broadway production of Of Mice and Men. *When she expressed concern about her portrayal of the character, Steinbeck wrote to her. In contrast to several critics' scathing interpretations of Curley's wife, Steinbeck paints a sympathetic portrait in this excerpt from his letter to Claire Luce.*

[Curley's wife] grew up in an atmosphere of fighting and suspicion. Quite early she learned that she must never trust any one but she was never able to carry out what she learned. A natural trustfulness broke through constantly and every time it did, she got hurt. Her moral training was most rigid. She was told over and over that she must remain a virgin because that was the only way she could get a husband. This was harped on so often that it became a fixation. It would have been impossible to seduce her. She had only that one thing to sell and she knew it.

Now, she was trained by threat not only at home but by other kids. And any show of fear or weakness brought an instant persecution. She learned she had to be hard to cover her fright. And automatically she became hardest when she was most frightened. She is a nice, kind girl and not a floozy. No man has ever considered her as anything except a girl to try to make. She has never talked to a man except in the sexual fencing conversation. She is not highly sexed particularly but knows instinctively that if she is to be noticed at all, it will be because some one finds her sexually desirable.

As to her actual sexual life—she has had none except with Curley and there has probably been no consummation there since Curley would not consider her gratification and would probably be suspicious if she had any. Consequently she is a little starved. She knows utterly nothing about sex except the mass of misinformation girls tell one another. If anyone—a man or a woman—ever gave her a break—treated her like a person—she would be a slave to that person. Her craving for contact is immense but she, with her background, is incapable of conceiving any contact without some sexual context. With all this—if you knew her, if you could ever break down the thousand little defenses she has built up, you would find a nice person, an honest person, and you would end up by loving her. But such a thing can never happen.

I hope you won't think I'm preaching. I've known this girl and I'm just trying to tell you what she is like. She is afraid of everyone in the world. You've known girls like that, haven't you? You can see them in Central Park on a hot night. They travel in groups for protection. They pretend to be wise and hard and voluptuous.

tries to "say" to little girls; but his brooding brother Quentin has meanwhile killed himself over the sexual turn which childhood love has taken, and his bachelor brother Jason has settled for lifelong hostility toward women. This troubled passage from innocence to carnal knowledge is as much Steinbeck's subject as Faulkner's; and like Faulkner, he sees it as a life-and-death ordeal.

Herein lies his strength and weakness in *Of Mice and Men:* for the passage from stroking rabbits to stroking genitals is both profoundly and ridiculously conceived. As literary zanies like Max Schulman and Steve Allen have been quick to see, Lennie's oft-repeated line, "Tell about the rabbits, George," comes perilously close to self-parody. Lifted only slightly out of context, it reduces the friendship farm to a bad sexual joke. As a sentimental alternative to the emptiness, divisiveness, and gross sexuality of bunkhouse life, it seems fair game for satire. But Steinbeck is never that simple. He is fascinated not by Lennie's innocent pleasures but by the low threshold which his innocent rages cross whenever he is thwarted. Consider Lennie's reaction when George imagines that striped cats may threaten his beloved rabbits: "You jus' let 'em try to get the rabbits," he says, breathing hard. "I'll break their God damn necks. I'll . . . I'll smash 'em with a stick.". . .

LENNIE'S INFANTILE REACTIONS

This frightening capacity for violence is what Lennie brings into the unsuspecting bunkhouse world: he carries within him, intact from childhood, that low threshold between rage and pleasure which we all carry within us into adulthood. But by adulthood we have all learned to take precautions which an idiot never learns to take. The force and readiness of our feelings continue: but through diversions and disguises, through civilized controls, we raise the threshold of reaction. This is the only real difference, emotionally, between Lennie and ourselves.

A great deal of Steinbeck's power as a writer comes, then, from his ability to bring into ordinary scenes of social conflict the psychological forcefulness of infantile reactions: his creation of Lennie in *Of Mice and Men is* a brilliant instance of that ability—so brilliant, in fact, that the social conflict in this compact tale tends to dissolve into the dramatic urgencies of Lennie's "fate.". . .

After killing Curley's wife, he flees to the grove near the Salinas River, as George has told him to. Back in his own element, he moves "as silently as a creeping bear," drinks like a wary animal, and thinks of living in caves if George doesn't want him any more. Then out of his head come two figures: his aunt Clara and (seven years before Mary Chase's *Harvey*) a giant rabbit. These figments of adult opinion bring all of George's petty righteousness to bear against him, shame him unmercifully, and threaten him with the only thing that matters: the loss of his beloved bunnies. Then out of the brush, like a third figment of Miltonic pettiness, comes George himself, as if to punish him once more for "being bad." But for Lennie . . . , badness is a matter of opinions and taboos, not of consequences and responsibilities. He doesn't care about Curley's wife, who exists for him now only as another lifeless animal. Nor does Steinbeck care about her except as she arrives at natural innocence; but he does care about that, and through Lennie, who possesses it in abundance, he is able to affirm his belief in the causeless, blameless animality of murder. Of course, he also believes in the responsibility of those who grasp the consequences of animal passion, and it is one of several paradoxes on which this novel ends that George comes humbly now to accept responsibility for such passions, comes not to punish Lennie, then, but to put him mercifully away, to let him die in full enjoyment of their common dream. So he asks him to face the Gabilan Mountains, which in *East of Eden* are said to resemble the inviting lap of a beloved mother; and, like a bedtime story or a prayer before execution—or better still, like both—together they recite the familiar tale of the friendship farm.

What makes this ending scary and painful and perplexing is the weight given to all that Lennie represents: if contradictory values are affirmed—blameless animality, responsible humanity, innocent longing, grim awareness—it is Lennie's peculiar mixture of human dreams and animal passions which matters most. George's newfound maturity is paradoxically an empty triumph: without Lennie he seems more like a horseless rider than a responsible adult. . . .

SWEET VIOLENCE

Steinbeck himself liked simple stories well enough to write straight allegories like *The Pearl* (1947). But chiefly he liked the puzzling kind. In *Tortilla Flat*, an otherwise comic novel, he shows, for instance, how Danny tires of the chivalric life and reverts to the "sweet violence" of outlawry. "Sweet violence" means something more here than the joys of boyish rebellion: it means delight in pulling the house down on one's own and other people's heads, which is what Danny does when the friendship dream proves insubstantial, and he pays with his life—and later, with his friends' help, with his house—for the pleasure of destroying it. Lennie too pays with his life for the pleasure of destructive rages; but he serves in this respect as an extension of his friend's desires: he is George Milton's idiot Samson, his blind avenger for the distastefulness of aggressive sexuality. Which may be why their friendship seems impossible from the first, why the pathos of their dream, and of its inevitable defeat, seems less important than the turbulence it rouses. Once more, "sweet violence" is the force which moves these characters, and which moves us to contemplate their puzzling fate.

By *East of Eden* Steinbeck would learn that rages generally follow from rejected love, that parental coldness or aloofness breeds violence in youthful hearts; and he would come also to accept sexuality as a vulnerable condition, a blind helplessness by which men and women may be "tricked and trapped and enslaved and tortured," but without which they would not be human. Oddly, he would create in Cathy Ames a monstrous projection of his old hostility toward women as exploiters of the sex impulse; and he would impose on her his own preternatural alertness to its selfish uses and his own fear of being absorbed and blinded by it in his youth. But by accepting sex now as a human need, he would redeem his Lennies and Dannys from outlawry and animality, and he would finally repair the ravages of sweet violence. *Of Mice and Men* remains his most compelling tribute to the force behind those ravages, "the most disturbing impulse humans have," as it moves a selfish master and his dancing bear to idiot rages. And once more it must be said to move us, too. For however contradictory it seems, our sympathy for these characters, indeed their love for each other, is founded more deeply in the humanness of that impulse than in its humanitarian disguises.

The Dream of a Male Utopia

Leland S. Person Jr.

Leland S. Person, a professor of English at Southern Illinois University at Carbondale, examines male-to-male relationships in *Of Mice and Men*. He believes that Steinbeck, through his portrayal of George and Lennie, explores an alternative manhood that challenges a patriarchal and capitalistic economy. The protagonists' dream of a male utopia features democratic cooperation and communalism without gender roles. Person concludes that Lennie's execution represents a return to traditional masculine life.

I want to examine *Of Mice and Men* within a pluralized discourse of masculinity—as a novel about men's relationships to other men. My reading will be "homosexual" in the sense that Robert K. Martin uses that term for male friendships in Melville's sea novels—for intimate same-sex relationships that do not necessarily involve genital sexuality.

Like Melville's novels, *Of Mice and Men* destabilizes conventional constructs of masculinity (patriarchal, heterosexual, and phallocentric) in order to explore alternative and subversive masculinities—indeed, a utopian dream founded on male bonding and a sublimated homosexual domesticity. *Of Mice and Men* resembles *Moby-Dick* in particular in marking out an imaginative space where male-to-male relationships can flourish. The novel opens at a "deep pool" in the Salinas River to which both ranch boys and tramps have beaten hard paths, and it is tempting to hear echoes of the "twentieth-eighth bather" section of Whitman's "Song of Myself" and of the sperm-squeezing scene in *Moby-Dick:* each scene suggesting the potential fluidity of male identity and male-to-male relationships. Martin notes two erotic forces in Melville's fiction: a "democratic eros" expressed "in male

From Leland S. Person Jr., *"Of Mice and Men*: Steinbeck's Speculations in Manhood," *Steinbeck Newsletter*, Winter/Spring 1995. Reprinted by permission.

friendship and . . . the celebration of a generalized seminal power not directed toward control and production; and a hierarchical eros expressed in social forms of male power." Whereas heterosexuality remains deeply rooted in subject-object power relationships, men who enter into homosexual relationships abdicate their roles in an "economy of power" over women and other men. Male friendships, such as the one between Ishmael and Queequeg, have the potential to subvert the economic, political, and sexual hierarchies that the normative heterosexual economy supports and to install cooperation rather than competition as the founding principle of male relationships.

A FRAGILE ECONOMY

Of Mice and Men positions its male characters between similar male sexual economies. The ranch economy is patriarchal and capitalistic—heterosexual and homosocial. The hierarchy descends from the boss through his son Curley to the jerkline skinner, Slim, and then to the workers. This fragile economy is homosocial in precisely the ways Eve Sedgwick describes in *Between Men,* because it depends upon the repression and sublimation of sexual desire, enabling men to get along and produce work. "Guys like us, that work on ranches, are the loneliest guys in the world," George tells Lennie. "They got no family. They don't belong no place. They come to a ranch an' work up a stake and then they go inta town and blow their stake, and the first thing you know they're poundin' their tail on some other ranch." Trapped within a vicious cycle of hard work, low wages, and wasteful expenditure, the "guys" who work the ranches are perpetually exploited and then, like Curley's dog, put out to a "pasture" they cannot own. Instead of saving for the future, the men spend their wages and their sexual selves in town at "old Suzy's place," where they can get a "flop" or "have a couple of shots." Heterosexual desire is carefully policed, in other words, relegated to the margins and incorporated into the capitalistic economy that governs the normative world of the ranch.

Curley's wife emphasizes the fragility of this economy because she crosses the carefully drawn lines between the ranch house and the bunk house, the owners and workers, and she exaggerates the fault lines between homosocial and heterosexual desires. A kind of outlaw virgin, Curley's wife is a "jail bait all set on the trigger," in George's terms. "Ranch with a bunch of guys on it ain't no place for a girl, specially like her," precisely because she threatens the homosocial working relationship between men. Instead of cooperating with one another, the men compete with each other—often violently, like Cain and Abel (see William Goldhurst and Peter Lisca), as Curley's compulsive effort to thwart his wife's relations with the men clearly shows. Or as she herself puts it, "You're all scared of each other . . . Ever' one of you's scared the rest is goin' to get something on you." Her appearance in the bunk house, her suggestive comment that "Nobody can't blame a person for lookin'," her open invitation of the male gaze as she throws her body forward— her actions require immediate interdiction and especially the proscription of Lennie's desire. "Listen to me, you crazy bastard," George tells Lennie. "Don't you even take a look at that bitch." Lennie's libido, or desire, seems largely narcissistic—expressed in petting behavior that seems more masturbatory than object-oriented.

Indeed, Lennie's preference for mice that he can keep in his pocket and pet with his thumb as he walks along pointedly suggests the masturbatory quality of his desire. Proscribing Lennie's attraction to Curley's wife enables the translation of Lennie's desire into vengeful violence—Curley's symbolic castration through the gloved hand he keeps "soft for his wife." In contrast to Ishmael's, Lennie's "squeeze of the hand" perverts the sort of homo-subjective bond that Melville realizes in *Moby-Dick,* converting desublimated desire into triangulated heterosexual and homosocial competition—dominant-subordinate mastery.

COMMUNALISM

In contrast, the "little house" dream that George and Lennie regularly invoke features democratic cooperation and communalism—an all-male version of the matriarchy that Warren Motley has detected in Ma Joad's role in *The Grapes of Wrath.* The two men collaborate dialogically to rehearse a mutual fantasy that subverts the conventionally entrepreneurial "ranch" ideal predicated on owner-worker and subject-object relationships. In effect, the two men share a single subjectivity in the act of collaboration. "You got it by heart," George tells Lennie. "You can do it yourself." But Lennie prefers to supplement George's rhythmical narrative with interpolations of his own—melting his desire into George's in a verbal analogy to Ishmael's mergence of body and mind with other men's in the big tub of sperm. "Someday," George begins, "we're gonna get the jack together and we're gonna have a little house and a couple of acres an' a cow and some pigs and—." *"An' live off the fatta the lan',"* Lennie shouts. "An' have *rabbits.* Go on, George! Tell about what we're gonna have in the garden and about the rabbits in the cages and about the rain in the winter and the stove."

Let me emphasize that what I am calling the homosexual dream is not genitally sexual. Indeed, it depends upon the sublimation of sexual energy in shared labor and home-making. "We'd have a little house an' a room to ourself," George says. "An' when we put in a crop, why we'd be there to take the crop up. We'd know what come of our planting." Lennie's sexuality, furthermore, is pointedly sublimated in stroking and petting—fantasmatically invested in tending rabbits, traditional symbols of unrestrained sexuality.

Not only does the homosexual dream dissolve competitive relationships, but it attracts and encourages other men to enter imaginatively into an all-male fantasy. Much like Melville, who discovered in the Ishmael-Queequeg bond a "radical potential for social reorganization, based on principles of equality, affection, and respect for the other" [according to Martin], Steinbeck explores alternative economic and social structures through the interdependent bond between George and Lennie. Not unlike Ishmael's revery in "the Squeeze of the Hand," when George and Lennie share the dream with Candy, "They all sat still, all bemused by the beauty of the thing, each mind was popped into the future when this lovely thing should come about." The stoop-shouldered, one-handed Candy volunteers to invest his $350 stake for the chance to "cook and tend the chickens and hoe the garden some"—his proposal reflecting the diversification of gender roles on which such a male utopia would be founded. "An' it'd be our own, an' nobody could can us," George says. "If we don't like a guy we can say 'Get the hell out,' and by God he's got to do it. An' if a fren' come along, why we'd have an extra bunk, an' we'd say, 'Why don't you spen' the night?' and by God he would." George and Lennie's homo-topic dream even dissolves racial barriers, as the crippled stable buck Crooks offers to "work for nothing—just his keep"—if he can be allowed to join them. "A guy needs somebody—to be near him," Crooks says. "Don't make no difference who the guy is, long's he's with you."

THE LENNIE-GEORGE RELATIONSHIP

George and Lennie's relationship obviously represents the emotional and thematic center of *Of Mice and Men*—microcosmically embodying the possibilities and the limitations of the world outside. Allegorical examples of partial manhood, the two men are opposites—"two parts of a single being," with Lennie representing "the Freudian id" and George "its controlling ego" [according to Lisca]. In the gendered terms that concern me here, however, it is more useful to look back to Plato's *Symposium* than to Freud. In Aristophanes' famous parable the sexes were originally three: man, woman, and the union of the two. Zeus cut man in two, however, leaving him "always looking for his other half," and Aristophanes imagines a plurality of potential pairings—homosexual as well as heterosexual. They who are "of the male," he says, "and while they are young, being slices of the original man, they hang about men and embrace them, and they are themselves the best of boys and youths because they have the most manly nature." Linking the greatest manliness with same-sex bonding, Aristophanes constructs a utopic masculine identity—a Super Manhood of sorts that *Of Mice and Men* intertextually explores.

A VIOLENT END

I want to focus on the execution that ends the novel—and violently destroys the possibility of intrapsychic union that Plato describes—because the ending bears so heavily on what I am calling Steinbeck's speculations in manhood. Positing the Lennie-George relationship in terms of investment and exchange helps show how personal relationships exemplify larger male-to-male economies—how the violent end of their relationship represents the death of the homosexual dream and, by default, the recovery of the patriarchal, capitalistic economy that the dream challenged.

Steinbeck carefully stages the murders in chapters 5 and 6 to emphasize the trade offs necessary in this complex sexual economy. When Lennie kills the puppy—in effect by loving it too much—he reasons that George will no longer let him tend the rabbits at their little place. One experience cancels the other. Similarly, as he shifts his attention to Curley's wife, he understands the "economic" consequences of his actions. "If George sees me talkin' to you," he tells her, "he'll give me hell," and even as she talks to him in a "passion of communication," Lennie strokes the dead puppy and thinks of his rabbits—exchanging heterosexual desire for auto-erotic fantasy and the homosexual utopia that promotes such innocent pleasure. The crisis comes, of course, when Lennie crosses the line between narcissistic and object-oriented, homosocial and heterosexual, desire. Lennie likes all soft things equally—a puppy, a mouse, a long-haired rabbit, a piece of velvet, a woman's hair—but petting Curley's wife subjects him to the same police action he had suffered in Weed when he grabbed the girl in the red dress. He kills Curley's wife so that George won't find out that he has "messed up" again, because "messing up" jeopardizes the homosexual dream he shares with George.

THE ROLE OF SLIM

That dream remains imperilled throughout the novel—questioned repeatedly by the other men. Slim, for example, tells George that "It jus' seems kinda funny a cuckoo like him and a smart little guy like you travelin' together." Although Emery considers Slim an androgynous character who integrates masculine and feminine attributes, she exaggerates Slim's femininity. Despite having hands "as delicate in their action as those of a temple dancer," Slim illustrates the successful masculinization of a male character along lines of classic manhood: "he moved with a majesty only achieved by royalty and master craftsmen"; he was "capable of killing a fly on the wheeler's butt with a bull whip without touching the mule"; there was a "gravity in his manner and a quiet so profound that all talk stopped when he spoke"; his "authority was so great that his word was taken on any subject, be it politics or love." If Lennie reflects a regressive, narcissistic stage of undistributed desire, Slim suggests the inscription of a stereotypically masculine self-image that writes over any potential androgyny. Slim's crucial part at the very end of the novel—consoling and leading George away from Lennie's dead body—reinforces the message that killing Lennie has meant killing and repressing the homosexual dream and the male bond.

George, like Slim, will eventually offer another example of successful repression. Earlier in the novel, in the bunkhouse, Slim had "fastened" his "calm, God-like eyes" on George while he described his relationship to Lennie. Under the gaze and sign of the patriarch, George adopts a "tone of confession," guiltily recalling the jokes he played on Lennie and, most importantly, the incident in Weed—the girl who cried rape when Lennie touched her red dress—both of these memories suggesting the dangers of unregulated sexuality. This tete-a-tete also foreshadows the final scene when Slim helps George compose himself, as well as compose the story of why he finally shot Lennie. Both scenes position George, as Sedgwick might say, "between men"—triangulating and mediating his desire between competing discourses of manhood.

The collective police action that closes the novel is designed to restore order to this male economy. Such vigilantism executes a final solution to the problem of destabilized manhood by eliminating the homosexual dream—and the homosexual dreamer. Not by accident does George position Lennie on his knees, tell him to stare vacantly "acrost the river" and imagine their little house, and then shoot him in the head. Despite the subtle references to Nazism in the images of the Luger and the behind-the-head execution, it would be going too far to compare George to the "fascist male" that Klaus Theweleit has anatomized in *Male Fantasies,* but executing Lennie does suggest a similar desire to purge the male self of an "other" manhood that threatens traditional masculine integrity. George is careful, therefore, to show the other men that he wasn't "in on" the murder of Curley's wife, and he tells Lennie just before he shoots him that he wants a life with "no mess"—alone and living "easy," taking his fifty bucks at the end of the month and going to a "cat house"—in other words, the traditional masculine life of the ranch and the other "guys."

A RETURN TO TRADITIONAL MASCULINITY

Where some critics see hope at the end of the novel—in the form of a new partnership between Slim and George—I see the recuperation of traditional masculinity and George's reincorporation into the normative heterosexual and homosocial economy of the ranch. "Now what the hell ya suppose is eatin' them two guys?"—Carlson's concluding rhetorical question—may be answered later for George and Slim via some return of the repressed, but immediately, it seems to me, this new pairing simply confirms George's place within a traditional patriarchal economy. "Me an' you'll go in an' get a drink," Slim says, and he leads George up toward the highway—away from the liminal space of the homosexual dream and into town, presumably to old Suzy's place, where "It's a hell of a lot of fun" and a guy doesn't even have to "want a flop." Unlike the fantasmatic bond between Lennie and George, this male bonding occurs within a framework of carefully invested heterosexual desire in which the homosocial and the heterosexual conspire to repress the homosexual fantasies George and Lennie once shared. In effect, the "squeeze of the hand" becomes a squeeze of the trigger that blows away the utopian homosexual dream.

Of Mice and Men Lacks Genuine Tragedy

Harry Thornton Moore

Harry Thornton Moore is the author of the first critical study of John Steinbeck, *The Novels of John Steinbeck*, published in 1939. Moore argues that *Of Mice and Men* is not a tragedy, and believes that the story suffers because it contains violence in tragedy's absence. He states that although the book has the roots of social tragedy, that is not enough to motivate the catastrophe at the end of the book. Likewise, while some of the characters can be called "tragic," they lack real tragic stature. This paucity, Moore adds, leaves the reader unprepared for Lennie's brutal death.

Steinbeck returned to his home valley for his next book, *Of Mice and Men*, the short novel that was to make him one of the most popular American authors of his time. The ranch where the story takes place is supposed to be about four and a half miles below Soledad, on the Salinas River.

An Unheralded Success

Of Mice and Men was written as an experiment. Steinbeck told his publisher not to disturb himself about the book if he didn't like it, and to send it back if it didn't interest him. But Pascal Covici was immediately enthusiastic about it and published it early in 1937. It was taken as a Book-of-the-Month Club selection and it entered the best-seller lists. Then as a play, adapted by Steinbeck with very little change, it ran for a crowded season on Broadway. The Drama Circle of the New York critics awarded it a prize for being the best play of the year. . . .

Structurally, the novel was from the first a play: it is divided into six parts, each part a scene—the reader may ob-

Excerpted from *The Novels of John Steinbeck: A First Critical Study* by Harry Thornton Moore (Chicago: Normandie House, 1939). Reprinted by permission of Mrs. Beatrice Moore.

serve that the action never moves away from a central point in each of these units. Steinbeck's manner of writing was coming over quite firmly to the dramatic. The process had begun in the latter part of *In Dubious Battle* (which the novelist John O'Hara once tried unsuccessfully to dramatize), where some of the most exciting happenings in the story take place offstage. After *Of Mice and Men* was published and the suggestion was made that it be prepared for the stage, Steinbeck said it could be produced directly from the book, as the earliest moving pictures had been produced. It was staged in almost exactly this way in the spring of 1937 by a labor-theater group in San Francisco, and although the venture was not a failure it plainly demonstrated to Steinbeck that the story needed to be adapted to dramatic form. The San Francisco *Chronicle*'s report of the performance admitted that the staged novel had power, though it "seems slightly ill at ease in the theater . . . Its climaxes need sharpening," for "some of the scenes end lamely, tapering off without the pointed tag-lines that might crystallize or intensify the action. And there are certain passages of dialogue that caused embarrassed titters in the audience; it would do the play no harm to leave these out altogether." But when Steinbeck transferred the story into final dramatic form for the New York stage he took 85% of his lines bodily from the novel. A few incidents needed juggling, one or two minor new ones were introduced, and some (such as Lennie's imaginary speech with his Aunt Clara at the end of the novel) were omitted. A Hollywood studio bought the film rights to *Of Mice and Men*, but the picture has not been made yet.

A SENSE OF DOOM

Although there are few descriptive passages in the novel *Of Mice and Men*, Steinbeck's presentation of ranch life has once again the gleam of the living. The people, human beings reduced to bareness of speech and thought and action, are on the sidetracks of the main line of western culture. They exist in a hard reality, but most of them are susceptible to dreams. Some of them are lost in a compensatory dream-image of themselves, others are set afire by the wish-dream of George and Lennie. But in one way or another all the dreams and some of the people (the good along with the bad) are smashed. The spirit of doom prevails as strongly as in the pages of Hardy or of Steinbeck's fellow-

Californian, Robinson Jeffers.

A writer deep in the lore of his own people feels (in many cases unconsciously) a folkways compulsive: the actual and mythical experience of his people helps to generate his material. But the final shaping of it depends upon the artist's own vision. Lennie in *Of Mice and Men* is cast up from the midst of us and we all know him. Baffled, unknowingly powerful, utterly will-less, he cannot move without a leader. And we also know many Georges, good-heartedly trying to help the Lennies of life muddle through; but all the while, despite their courage and good intentions, none too certain of themselves. John Steinbeck sees them as unable to prevent their charges (and often themselves) from steering into catastrophe. In book after book his protagonists, tragic or comic, are shattered, and it goes hardest with those who had the brightest dreams. It is disturbing to find so many of these likeable heroes going down so consistently in spiritual defeat or meeting with a brutal death.

No Tragedy

Violence without tragedy: that is the weakness of this book. Socially considered, most of the people are what could legitimately be called "tragic," but there is no tragedy as we understand the word in reference to literature. On the social side, we have George's ritual of dreaming aloud with Lennie, which begins with this incantation:

> Guys like us, that work on ranches, are the loneliest guys in the world. They got no family. They don't belong no place. They come to a ranch an' work up a stake and then they go into town and blow their stake, and the first thing you know they're poundin' their tail on some other ranch. They ain't got nothing to look ahead to . . .

and continues:

> With us it ain't like that. We got a future. We got somebody to talk to that gives a damn about us. We don't have to sit in no bar room blowin' in our jack jus' because we got no place else to go . . . Someday—we're gonna get the jack together and we're gonna have a little house and a couple of acres an' a cow and some pigs . . .

This has roots of social tragedy, despite the sentimental manner of its statement. (Steinbeck once said he writes this way because he is a sentimental guy.) George and Lennie and Candy and Crooks and some of the others are caught in this situation, they are lonely and homeless and yearning.

But the social tragedy never really gets beyond that static proposition: its potentials are never exercised. It affords a background but it doesn't motivate the catastrophe.

An Abrupt Ending

On the literary side there is no authentic tragedy, which comes out of character. There is no basis for it. Even if we slur over the criticism that Lennie is a poor choice for a central figure in the story because from the start the odds against him are too great—even if we get beyond this and admit George as the true protagonist, we still don't find tragedy. George is no more than pathetic. He attracts sympathy because he has to lose his friend Lennie, to whom he has been so loyal, and whom he has to kill at the last in order to save him from the others. But because this isn't genuine tragedy it gives the reader a brutal shock when George kills Lennie, and it cannot be anything else no matter how many little tricks have been used throughout the story to prepare us for Lennie's death. One of the most noticeable of these is the obvious comparison of Lennie with a worthless old dog that must be shot, as Lennie must be at the last.

An Artificial Effect

It is true that Elizabethan tragedy ended with corpses and horror, and one doesn't protest against them when they are necessary ingredients to tragedy: it is the misuse of corpses and horror that is objectionable. It can become a trick. All that side of the *Of Mice and Men* story is crude and shoddy. The writing comes to reflect this, and although there are occasionally excellent terse descriptive passages, projections of atmosphere as well as superb descriptions of physical actions, the prose finally comes to seem as if it were stretched too tight—it gives an effect of bright artificiality. The projection is really too bare for narrative; since the main story is so slight it should have been filled in more at the sides. Its very narrowness emphasizes the awkward attempt to resolve pathos by brutality.

Fifteen of Steinbeck's short stories (three of them being parts of *The Red Pony,* previously mentioned) were published in September 1938 under the title of *The Long Valley.* These stories give something of a resume of Steinbeck's career, as several of them date back for a few years and others are more recent, two never having appeared in print before.

The stories are mostly experimental; Steinbeck had been for a long time working out a theory of subconscious symbolism, by which certain elements of the rhythm and certain hidden symbols prepare the reader's unconsciousness for the ultimate effect of the story. Great literature does this automatically—when a too deliberate attempt is made to achieve such means, the result is often a failure, as we have seen in looking over *Of Mice and Men.*

CHAPTER 4

Of Mice and Men: The Play

The Play Accentuates the Consummate Art of Steinbeck

Burton Rascoe

Journalist, critic, and author Burton Rascoe was among the first to give serious critical examination to Steinbeck's fiction. This colorful essay was originally printed in the March 1938 issue of the *English Journal.* In his laudatory reading, Rascoe compares the play version of *Of Mice and Men* to a Sophoclean tragedy. He also comments on Steinbeck's ability to generate true compassion for the misfits of life. That the imbecilic Lennie merits the reader's sympathy is testament to Steinbeck's narrative skill, Rascoe believes. Interestingly, Rascoe reveals personal conversations with Steinbeck in an attempt to illuminate the author's life philosophy.

On the evening of November 23, 1937, an aesthetic miracle was performed on the stage of the Music Box Theatre in New York City. It was the occasion of the first presentation of John Steinbeck's play *Of Mice and Men.* The more literate portion of the reading public had become familiar with the story or theme of the play because *Of Mice and Men* had first appeared in book form as a novel and had met with great critical acclaim, and, fortunately, this critical acclaim had been followed by purchases of the book in large quantities. . . .

I am very glad Mr. Steinbeck did not attend the opening performance of *Of Mice and Men* in New York and that he has not, as yet, seen a performance of the play. For, although the play was an instantaneous hit and although it drew from the drama critics the most gravely and warmly worded notices of praise that have been accorded any native drama since *Tobacco Road* (and hence is likely to enjoy a run as extended as the Erskine Caldwell drama), a distressingly large

Excerpted from Burton Rascoe, "John Steinbeck," *English Journal,* March 1938.

part of the audience on the opening night took the tragic, heart-breaking lines of George and Lennie to be comedy. They laughed outrageously when tears should have been streaming down their faces. They appeared to think that the lumbering, dimwitted, pathetic Lennie was supposed to be funny. Village idiots laughing at the village idiot all over again. I am told that this laughter at the wrong places occurs during at least part of the first act at every performance.

COMPASSION FOR MISFITS

But the consummate art of Steinbeck conquers every time even the more insensitive elements of a New York theater audience before the first act is over. Compassion for the misfits of life, for those who are handicapped by the imponderables of heredity and environment and for those who are warped physically and emotionally, is so deeply and so understandingly felt and expressed by Steinbeck that, before the curtain comes down on the first act, the light, superficially cynical mood of the less sensitive members of the audience has changed, and pity and wonder has taken possession of them.

This is the miracle I referred to in the opening sentence of this discourse.

It seemed to me after my first reading, subsequent rereadings, and careful analysis of the novel, *Of Mice and Men,* that Steinbeck as a literary artist had deliberately posed for himself the most difficult problem conceivable to a writer of fiction and that he had resolved it in a Sophoclean manner, that is, without poetic or rhetorical fault. He had even done a braver thing than Sophocles had done (though, please, let no one be so silly and so supercilious as to imagine that, in my saying this, I am comparing Sophocles and Steinbeck to the disadvantage of Sophocles or even that I am ranking Steinbeck as remotely in the class of Sophocles: he may be, before he is finished, a greater poetic dramatist than Sophocles, for he strives to learn the most delicate nuances and the most meaningful emphases of—in the Aristotelian sense— the arts of poetry and rhetoric; but he is thirty-eight years old, and Sophocles was only twenty-eight when he triumphed over the long preeminent tragic poet, Aeschylus, by writing *Antigone;* so, in order to be classed with Sophocles, Steinbeck has much ground, in little time, to cover). I am talking about a writing problem. Sophocles chose to treat in poetic and dramatic form the legends already familiar to the Athenian audiences who had witnessed tragic dramas since the days before Aeschylus. Steinbeck, on the other hand, chose as the most important character of his novel, and of his play, *Of Mice and Men,* a believable contemporary figure—a man who would be described on any police docket or in a detective's dossier as a sexual pervert or degenerate and in almost any psychiatrist's case history as, probably, a man afflicted with gigantism, with an abnormally low I.Q., unusual thyroid deficiency, excessive pituitary secretion with resulting imbalance, a tactile fetish, psychic and/or physical impotence, and with improperly functioning adrenals which caused him in moments of fear to act destructively without intention—and Steinbeck chose to, and *did,* make this monstrosity a sympathetic figure, one whom you, if you had heart in you, would regard with all the despair but also with all the affection with which the giant Lennie is regarded by his bindle-stiff guardian and companion, the more astute and intelligent George.

In the novel and in the play the relationship between George and Lennie is a paradigm of all the nonphysical, nonsexual (let us use the so tritely inadequate and now almost meaningless word "spiritual" to help out in indicating the meaning) emotions, concerns, and aspirations in the world. George has toward Lennie the tenderness and the protective instinct which some of even the most hard-bitten and most hard-boiled have toward the helpless, the maimed, the dependent. A lonely, itinerant bindle-stiff, a migratory ranch hand, barley bucker, mule skinner, fruit picker, and general handy man, without a home or family, George has encountered and embraced a responsibility, a social responsibility, a humanitarian responsibility. It is to take care of, protect, save from hurt, the dim-witted, loyal, and devoted Lennie.

George nags and rags Lennie at times like a distracted, exasperated harridan wife; scolds him like a long-suffering mother whose child is a constant worry and trial. He gives way at times to eloquent fancies as to how much more enjoyable, unconstrained, and livable life would be if he were only free—if he didn't have Lennie as a burden, a yoke, a ball and chain to hamper him. But as George speaks and as his character becomes plain, you know that life would be wholly meaningless and empty for him without Lennie to take care of. And he has his emotional recompense in

Lennie's pathetic and doglike devotion to him, a loyalty so great and so intense that Lennie's weak brain scarcely comes alive except where George is concerned—when George is angry with him, when George is planning a future for them wherein they will have a little farm of their own and won't be subject to the whims of bosses or to the seasonal variations in employment, or when harm seems to threaten George.

The never-quite-realized, too often tragically shattered dreams of men toward an ideal future of security, tranquillity, ease, and contentment runs like a Greek choral chant throughout the novel and the play, infecting, enlivening, and ennobling not only George and Lennie but the crippled, broken-down ranch hand, Candy, and the twisted-back Negro stable buck, Crooks, who begs to come in on the plan George has to buy a little farm. Lennie is so enthralled by the prospect that he begs George to tell the story over and over again:

LENNIE (*pleading*): Come on, George. . . . Tell me! Please! Like you done before.

. . . .

GEORGE: Guys like us that work on ranches is the loneliest guys in the world. They ain't got no family. They don't belong no place. They come to a ranch and then they go into town and blow their stake. And then the first thing you know they're poundin' their tail on some other ranch. They ain't got nothin' to look ahead to.

LENNIE (*delightedly*): That's it, that's it! Now tell how it is with us.

GEORGE (*still almost chanting*): With us it ain't like that. We got a future. We got somebody to talk to that gives a damn about us. We don't have to sit in no barroom blowin' our jack, just because we got no place else to go. If them other guys gets in jail, they can rot for all any body gives a damn.

LENNIE (*who cannot restrain himself any longer; bursts into speech*): But not us! And why? Because . . . because I got you to look after me . . . and you got me to look after you. . . . And that's why! (*He laughs.*) Go on, George!

GEORGE: You got it by heart. You can do it yourself.

LENNIE: No, no. I forget some of the stuff. Tell about how it's gonna be.

GEORGE: Some other time.

LENNIE: No, tell how it's gonna be!

GEORGE: Okay. Some day we're gonna get the jack together and we're gonna have a little house and a couple of acres and a cow and some pigs and. . . .

LENNIE (*shouting*): And live off the fat of the land! And have rabbits. Go on, George! Tell about what we're gonna have in the garden. And about the rabbits in the cages. Tell about the rain in the winter . . . and about the stove and how thick the cream is on the milk, you can hardly cut it. Tell about that, George!

GEORGE: Why don't you do it yourself—you know all of it!

LENNIE: It ain't the same if I tell it. Go on now. How I get to tend the rabbits.

(GEORGE *continues to elaborate the story of the dream place.*)

And now you must observe that Steinbeck has compassion without maudlinity, sentiment without sentimentality, a stern, realistic, very observant and deductive sense about the realities and about the consequences in a chain of causes. Anyone with any deductive sense at all needs to read only five pages of the novel *Of Mice and Men* to discover the "plot," to know what is going to happen. The intelligent reader knows that poor Lennie is going to "do a bad thing again" as he did before when he wanted to stroke a girl's dress (and that was all he wanted to do), and the girl got frightened and screamed because she thought she was being attacked, and Lennie and George had to run away and hide in a swamp in water up to their necks to escape the mob that was going to lynch Lennie.

You know that *this* time Lennie, who likes to stroke soft things and who has killed a pet mouse because his hands are so strong and he is so dumb, is going to kill a girl, unintentionally, because of all the things wrong in his disordered brain. The impatient, plot-minded reader doesn't have to turn to the back of the book to see how it comes out. Steinbeck tells you, in effect, in the first five pages just about how it is "going to come out."

STEINBECK: A MASTER OF NARRATION

And that is his terrific moral. Also it is his gambit to the reader to prove his power as a convincing and enthralling narrator. The reader who, having read that far, fails to go on, is a reader whose mentality is equal only to, and has been conditioned by, very bad, tricky, detective stories, which have no true relation to literature any more than have crossword puzzles, or, indeed, any more than crossword puzzles have (as they are alleged to have) to the increase of the vocabulary you would ordinarily, or potentially, use.

You see, Steinbeck not only indicates to the sentient reader in those first five pages that Lennie is going "to do a bad thing" unintentionally: he also indicates to the sentient reader that Lennie will have to die for it this time and, also,

that it is highly necessary and just that Lennie should die.
For Lennie's condition is an inimical and destructive force.
It is a condition he is not responsible for. It is something he
cannot help. One can have all the feeling for him in the

ARTFUL DESCRIPTIONS

*Steinbeck is arguably the master of evocative descriptions
of the California landscape.* Of Mice and Men *opens with
the following passage, which sets a tone that is maintained
throughout the book. Also noteworthy is the way in which
Steinbeck establishes a chord of tension when man intrudes on
the peaceful scene.*

A few miles south of Soledad, the Salinas River drops in close
to the hillside bank and runs deep and green. The water is
warm too, for it has slipped twinkling over the yellow sands
in the sunlight before reaching the narrow pool. On one side
of the river the golden foothill slopes curve up to the strong
and rocky Gabilan mountains, but on the valley side the water
is lined with trees—willows fresh and green with every
spring, carrying in their lower leaf junctures the debris of the
winter's flooding; and sycamores with mottled, white, recum-
bent limbs and branches that arch over the pool. On the sandy
bank under the trees the leaves lie deep and so crisp that a
lizard makes a great skittering if he runs among them. Rabbits come out of the brush to sit on the sand in the evening,
and the damp flats are covered with the night tracks of 'coons,
and with the spread pads of dogs from the ranches, and with
the split-wedge tracks of deer that come to drink in the dark.

There is a path through the willows and among the
sycamores, a path beaten hard by boys coming down from the
ranches to swim in the deep pool, and beaten hard by tramps
who come wearily down from the highway in the evening to
jungle-up near water. In front of the low horizontal limb of a
giant sycamore there is an ash pile made by many fires; the
limb is worn smooth by men who have sat on it.

Evening of a hot day started the little wind to moving
among the leaves. The shade climbed up the hills toward the
top. On the sand banks the rabbits sat as quietly as little gray,
sculptured stones. And then from the direction of the state
highway came the sound of footsteps on crisp sycamore
leaves. The rabbits hurried noiselessly for cover. A stilted
heron labored up into the air and pounded down river. For a
moment the place was lifeless, and then two men emerged
from the path and came into the opening by the green pool.

world—but Candy in the second act of the play has an old, rheumatic, blind, crippled dog, smelly with age and disease, of whom Candy is very fond because this old dog is the only thing left to Candy on which, or on whom, to lavish human affection, warmth, and care; and Candy has to carry the old dog around in his arms until the dog's disintegrating smell so permeates the bunkhouse that the other ranch hands can no longer stand it, and they have to persuade Candy, with the utmost kindness and consideration, to let them put the old dog out of his misery.

Therein, truly, is a displayed sense of the *lacrimae rerum* [pity for misfortune] of which John Steinbeck is a master. For, when the posse is seeking poor Lennie to string him up and "blow his guts out," as the egoistically inflamed and sadistic leader of the posse demands, George humors Lennie by telling him again about the place they are going to have. He tells it all over, word for word, with promptings by Lennie, who knows it all but wants to hear it from George. He tells it to keep Lennie in ecstasy until the shouts and other noises disclose that the posse is near upon them. Then:

> GEORGE: And you get to tend the rabbits!
> LENNIE (*giggling with happiness*): And live on the fat o' the land!
> GEORGE. Yes. (LENNIE *turns his head. Quickly*): Look over there, Lennie. Like you can really see it.
> (GEORGE *pulls* CARLSON's *Luger from his side pocket and fires at the base of* LENNIE's *brain, to put him out of his misery, just as* CARLSON *had told* CANDY *he could put* CANDY's *old dog out of his misery and the dog wouldn't know or feel it, because the bullet would go right into the base of the brain.*)

After that, it seems to me that many of the "hard-boiled" writers who imitate Hemingway's hard-boilism (and including Hemingway who now imitates himself) are like just so many Lennies parroting what George has said, except that their George was about as unimaginative in the brainpan as Lennie and even much more undeveloped, however facile and neat were the hard-boiled word patterns their George was able to patter out. The George of Steinbeck's novel and play was hard-bitten and hard-boiled; but he had imagination, a sense of reality, true compassion, and the dream of life.

Steinbeck abhors and abjures the tag "mystic" which some critics have used in describing him. He is deeply concerned with the problem of Good and Evil, not in any conventional, moral, or philosophical sense but as phenomena in life and as animating principles in life. I have heard him use no word indicating the nature of his beliefs and intimations; but I should vaguely describe them as comprising a curious, very modern Manicheanism, derived perhaps in part from the Indians of the West Coast he has known since boyhood, from acute observation of cause and effect operating among primitive or untutored men, and from a frank facing of the evidence of his own hidden resources of mind and will. Although I have not heard him mention the late Mary Austin or give any evidence of having read her studies of the mind and will, it occurred to me that his psychic beliefs and convictions are probably akin to those of Mrs. Austin. Mrs. Austin believed that will, thought, and emotion are forces that are immediate, dynamic, and kinetic and that they can bring about definite ends, for good or evil, without the employment of any physical means whatever.

CONVERSATIONS WITH STEINBECK

It would appear from a long conversation at my house which followed upon Steinbeck's bland, resolute affirmation that what is commonly called witchcraft and the "hexing" of one person by another person is not a superstition but a fairly common and attestable fact. It is, he says, merely the operation of the kinetic and highly destructive emotion of hate. This is, he says, a disturbing and terrible fact. He says that he knew of a man who had reason to hate another man greatly and did so hate him with such concentrated emotion that he was able to say to that man, "You are going to die next Tuesday. At 2:15 next Tuesday you are going to step in front of a truck." And the man did step in front of a truck at 2:15 the following Tuesday and was killed. Steinbeck denied that this was hypnotism, although he believes that all of us daily perform hypnotism and are subjects of hypnotism almost daily in degrees depending upon the force unconsciously exercised upon us, our resistance to it, and upon the strength of our own will and purpose.

He said that he was mortally afraid of hate and that he never wanted to hate anyone or have anyone hate him—very much. The only defense against concentrated hate, he said, was immediate surrender, capitulation; and this must take the form of humility, benevolence, friendliness. The only way to combat hate is to remove from within yourself the reasons for this hate; only thus can you disarm the one who hates you; only thus can you render the terrible force of his hate impotent. "If I knew a man hated me a great deal," he said, "I would try to make friends with him; if I had done him harm I would try to undo that harm quickly. I wouldn't try to hate him back, no, no, because then the only reason I would have for hating him was because he hated me, and that isn't reason enough to generate any strong, counteracting emotion. This would only intensify his hate and he might take it into his head to will disaster or death upon me."

Presently I perceived that Steinbeck's metaphysics was having to do, in a language and ratiocination of his own, with what in the Greek consciousness was the high sin of *hubris* or arrogance or insolence and its consequences. In Greek tragedy there are degrees and kinds of *hubris* each with degrees and kinds of punishment extending up to dire suffering and disaster, the reasons for which the victim in his *hubris* or unwarranted and exaggerated self-conceit cannot figure out; he does not know why he has offended the gods; but the audience knows; he thought too well of himself and so aroused hatred by insolence without even knowing he was insolent and so brought punishment upon himself.

In *Of Mice and Men* Steinbeck's thematic intention, not wholly obvious, was, in a way, to expound the complete nonmorality of Nature in her physical aspects and of the morality of expediency that must necessarily arise from Nature's blundering. The giant imbecile was certainly not responsible for being what he was, and nothing could right the bungling of Nature, and yet this giant imbecile, fully meriting our pity, sympathy, and tenderness, must be killed; for society cannot permit, out of pity, the dumb, destructive force of bungling, nonmoral Nature to operate.

The Use of Candy on the Stage

Robert Cardullo

Robert Cardullo presented the following paper at the University of Florida Department of Classics Comparative Drama Conference in March 1981. In his analysis of the play *Of Mice and Men*, Cardullo emphasizes the importance of the subplot featuring Candy. First, once his dog is dead, Candy is in the same precarious position as the imbecilic Lennie. Second, Candy's strategic placement in the story outlines the deep and tragic love George has for Lennie, with whom he shares the dream of farm ownership. Even after Lennie's death, George could still buy the farm with Candy, who has offered his money and his labor for the chance to be their partner. By rejecting Candy, Cardullo maintains, George is really rejecting the dream of the farm, proving that for George, being on a farm with Lennie was more important than simply being on a farm.

It has often been suggested that the "Candy and his dog" subplot in *Of Mice and Men* (1937) is too much, that it is a typical example of Steinbeck's heavyhandedness or overfondness for parallels. In fact, some student and workshop productions of the play omit the dog entirely. But Candy and the dog are very important to the action. The point of Carlson's shooting of the dog—who is old and blind and smells—is not to make an easy parallel with George's shooting of Lennie, as Peter Lisca and Harry T. Moore seem to think. It is not the dog so much who is in the same position as the imbecilic Lennie; it is the shooting of the dog that places *Candy* in the same position. Once he does not have his dog to look after anymore, Candy realizes the precariousness of his own position on the ranch: he is without one hand, and therefore only able to

Excerpted from Robert Cardullo, "On the Road to Tragedy: The Function of Candy in *Of Mice and Men*," in *All the World: Drama Past and Present*, edited by Karelisa Hartigan. Copyright ©1982 by University Press of America. Reprinted by permission of the author and publisher.

"swamp out" bunkhouses, and he is fast approaching senility.

To stress the similarity between Candy's position and Lennie's, Steinbeck has Candy, and no other character in the play, treat Lennie as his mental equal. George never explains Lennie's condition to Candy as he does, say, to Slim. Candy tells Lennie about the "figuring" he has been doing, about how, if they go about it right, they can make some money on the rabbits they propose to have on their farm; but Lennie for his part can think of nothing except petting the rabbits. Candy *sounds* like Lennie when he says, "We gonna have a room to ourselves. We gonna have a dog and chickens. We gonna have green corn and maybe a cow." And he acts like Lennie when he comes into Crooks's room in the barn. He only says, "This is the first time I ever been in [Crooks's] room"; he seems honestly not to realize that the reason for this is that, as Crooks says, "Guys don't come in a

---

STEINBECK AND CENSORSHIP

Steinbeck's use of profanity has fueled debate about his books' suitability for young readers. Specifically, Of Mice and Men *is among the most frequently banned books in the United States. In this excerpt from the* Steinbeck Newsletter, *Richard Hoffstedt describes recent attempts to ban Steinbeck's writing.*

According to the September 1990 issue of *Writer's Digest,* the top three "Most Banned Books in the United States"—those "most often removed from library and school bookshelves"— are *The Catcher in the Rye, The Grapes of Wrath,* and *Of Mice and Men.* Faulkner, Hemingway, and all of our other Nobel Prize winners in literature did not make the top ten. What did Steinbeck say in these two magnificent novels that has been so disturbing for over fifty years?

Recent attempts to ban these books are aimed at school and library boards, so it is young readers who are being singled out as the group most in need of having their reading material reduced to a "safe" list of acceptable authors—writers who will not stimulate young people to think critically. According to People For the American Way or PAW (a group of concerned citizens headed by TV producer and director Norman Lear whose objective is to protect the First Amendment), most demands for removal of books from libraries and teacher-required reading lists come from parents who belong to a

colored man's room." Yet he has been on the ranch for a long time, and so has Crooks.

Like Lennie, then, Candy needs someone to run his affairs, to make the rest of his life easier and more congenial. He needs George. Slim promises Candy a puppy from his bitch Lulu's litter to compensate for the shooting of his sheep dog, but Candy never gets that puppy, and he never asks for it. Lennie can attempt to look after a pup, because he has George to look after him. Candy is in search of a home for himself; he cannot afford, at this point, to give one to a dog. But Candy, finally, is not Lennie, and George will not team up with him after Lennie is gone. Candy does not accompany the men in their hunt for Lennie, after Curley's wife is found dead in the barn. He stays on the ranch, all alone, deserted, as it were, by everyone, even as he will be by George, after Lennie has been shot. Candy's "Poor bastard,"

---

variety of so-called family and/or religious groups. In 1989 "The West [led] in total number of incidents . . . and California accumulated more incidents than any other state." The threads that always seem to weave through the objections of fundamentalists are strong, "anti-Christian" language as well as anything they see as being too sexual.

Let's look at some of the recent attempts to ban Steinbeck's writings. . . . Most were found in various daily papers monitored by PAW. In Escondido, California, according to the PAW 1988–'89 Report, "the head of the Christian Voters League, led by Reverend Billy Falling, demanded that the school board adopt a policy barring teachers from requiring oral readings of literature that contains profanity or takes God's name in vain." One of his specific objections was to *The Grapes of Wrath.* In Berrien Springs, Michigan, a group of local ministers objected to *Of Mice and Men* being taught in a 10th grade English class. According to one minister, "If it contains profanity or vulgar words, it is bad junk and should not be in our schools and I don't care if it is considered a classic." (This last quotation was documented in the *Muskegon Chronicle* on August 31, 1989 and appeared in many of our nation's journals.) In Sedro-Wooley, Washington, according to PAW, objections were raised to using *Of Mice and Men* in a ninth grade English class because of its obscene language.

said to Curley's dead wife, lying in the hay, once the men have left, could just as well be applied to himself as to Lennie or Curley's wife.

TRAGIC LOVE

There is tragedy in *Of Mice and Men.* . . . That is why Candy is in the play. It is so understated, however, one barely notices it. The tragedy really has nothing to do with George's shooting of Lennie per se. As film critic Otis Ferguson once remarked, "I have never been quite sure that George shouldn't have shot [Lennie] before the story began." Ferguson was not trying to be funny. His meaning was that Lennie is a "case" on the loose, and that his killing of Curley's wife, and being shot for it by George, could just as easily have happened "before" the play or "after" it as during it. Steinbeck "arranges" for it to happen during the play, after they meet Candy. Is this so we can feel sorry for poor Lennie, as many believe? I don't think so. His point was that George deeply loved this "idiot," with the result that he always wanted Lennie to be with him in his travels and his work. Once he shoots Lennie, George can still get the farm with Candy if he wants to (recall that it is largely Candy's money that will buy the farm, and Candy is still more than willing). But he declines, which proves that being in one safe place *with Lennie* was more important to him than simply being in one safe place. He elects to continue living the hard life of a ranchhand rather than settle down to life on a small farm with Candy. George can have a better life, yet turns it down. Unquestionably he will suffer more on the road, without Lennie, than on the farm, without Lennie. He never gives himself a chance to, in his words, "get used to" Candy. This is not simple pathos. It approximates tragedy because it suggests *George loved Lennie too much,* that he was unnaturally attached to him; but also—and here's the rub—that this was the only way he could ever have put up with (and done so much for) one such as Lennie in the first place, by developing an unnatural attachment to him. It suggests he is sentencing himself to the same fate eventually as other "guys that go round on the ranches alone": he will not have any fun, and after a while he will get mean. He lives but the fate spoken for him by Crooks: this is the accompaniment to the tragic inevitability of the play. Crooks says, "I seen hundreds of men come by on the road and on the ranches, bindles on their back and that same damn thing in their head. Hundreds of 'em. They come and they quit and they go on. And every damn one of 'em is got a little piece of land in his head. And never a goddamn one of 'em gets it." The implication is that George will have that little piece of land in his head once again, after months of working hard and blowing his money in "cathouses" and pool rooms, and that is when he will become "tragically aware" of how he really lost his land—not by losing Lennie, but by rejecting Candy—and how he will never be given the chance to get it again. Like Othello, he will have loved not wisely, but too well. Like any other tragic hero's, his awareness will be one of acceptance more than self-reproach.

A SYMPATHETIC PORTRAIT OF GEORGE

So while the play underlines the bond of friendship that existed between George and Lennie (a bond difficult for some in today's audiences to accept on any but homosexual grounds), it also makes that bond responsible for George's rash decision not to buy the small farm with Candy's assistance. We are in full sympathy with George when he makes his decision, nevertheless we cannot help but feel at the same time that he is making a mistake, that he is doing something noble yet horrible and wasteful, of Candy's life as well as his own. Candy's "Poor bastard" this time applies to George, whom we leave alone, with the dead Lennie, at the end of the play.

George is not especially articulate or self-examining. He has never married. Lennie is his emotional attachment. He does not make many friends or ask many questions. Candy is his "attachment" to the ranch: Candy first fills him in about the Boss, then about Curley and his wife, Crooks, Slim. Candy, with his life savings, becomes George's way out of ranch life. With Lennie dead, he becomes potentially George's emotional attachment. He is, in the end, the embodiment or articulation of all the aims and emotions that George in his sorrow is oblivious to, but which will arise to haunt him again. Thus Steinbeck ends scenes one and two of Act III with Candy and George in the same position: haunching over dead bodies. They are in the same position, in need of each other, but inalterably separated. And finally they are silent, one in memory of the other.

Like George, the play's tragedy is quiet. Like George, the play seems to focus more on Lennie than its own life, that is, more than anything else, on its identification with George. It sacrifices attention to him for attention to Lennie, on the way *he* would have done it. That is why, unfairly, *Of Mice and Men* has too often been called nothing more than a work of sentiment. It is much more than that. We come to George's tragedy the long way around, through Candy. Lennie is not diminished by this; rather, George and Candy are elevated.

Steinbeck's Use of a Play Format Restricts the Development of the Story

Howard Levant

According to Howard Levant, from the first, *Of Mice and Men* was structured as a play. Levant contends that *Of Mice and Men* is flawed in that Steinbeck cannot explore complex human motives and relationships because the novel's play format limits the development of the story to visible action. The activity, Levant notes, is too complex for the extreme simplification of structure and materials required by this form. Thus, he concludes, the story remains a parable. Levant is the author of *The Novels of John Steinbeck: A First Critical Study*, from which this selection is excerpted.

It would seem that [*Of Mice and Men*] was intended to function as a play, and Steinbeck did not alter the novel in any essential during the tinkering in preparation for the New York stage production.... And clearly the novel does "play": Characters make entrances and exits; plainly indicated parallels and oppositions that are characteristic of the drama exist in quantity and function as they should; suspense is maintained; characters are kept uncomplicated and "active" in the manner of stage characterization; since there is little internal or implicit development, events depend on what is said or done in full view; the locale is restricted mainly to one place; the span of time is brief; the central theme is stated and restated—the good life is impossible because humanity is flawed—and in itself is deeply poignant, as Steinbeck had defined a play-novelette theme. In short, I do not see how *Of Mice and Men* could meet more completely the specifications of a play-novelette as Steinbeck listed them. If critics have been displeased with *Of Mice and Men,* as Steinbeck was, the trouble cannot lie in the application of the theory but in the assumption that inspired the theory. I shall explore this point in detail.

OF MICE AND MEN REMAINS A PARABLE

As a dramatic structure, *Of Mice and Men* is focused on Lennie and occurs within the context of the bunkhouse and the ranch. Within these confines, Steinbeck develops theme and countertheme by exploring the chances for the good life against the flawed human material that Lennie symbolizes most completely and the code of rough justice that most people accept. Even this initial, limited statement points to the central difficulty in the novel. The "well-made" dramatic form that Steinbeck . . . did construct in *Of Mice and Men* is conducive to abstraction because it is limited to visible action. Lennie is limited in much the same way. As a huge, powerful, semi-idiot who kills when he is frightened or simply when he is thoughtless, Lennie is a reduction of humanity to the lowest common denominator. It may be possible to construct a parable out of so limited a structure and materials, but it is impossible to handle complex human motives and relationships within those limits. *Of Mice and Men* is successful to the extent that it remains a parable, but the enveloping action is more complex than the parable form can encompass.

Lennie is the most fully realized character, yet he is presented necessarily as a personification, an exaggerated, allegorized instance of the division between mind and body; the sketch that is Lennie is incapable of conveying personality. The other characters are personified types rather than realized persons. Though less pathetic than Lennie, they do not have his moral impact. In short, every structural device except personification is sacrificed to highlight Lennie's moral helplessness. The sacrifice is much too great. It thins out the parable. The stripped language furthers this effect of extreme thinness. For example, Lennie's one friend, George, is not a realized man but a quality that complements Lennie's childlike innocence. George fills out Lennie's pattern to complete a whole man. He is a good man, motivated to protect Lennie because he realizes that Lennie is the reverse image of his own human nature. George is a representation of humanity that (unlike Lennie) is aware of evil. . . .

EXTREME SIMPLIFICATION

Everything in the development of the novel is designed to contribute to a simplification of character and event.

The opening scene of the green pool in the Salinas River promises serenity, but in the final scene the pool is the background for Lennie's violent death. George's initial hope that Lennie can hide his flawed humanity by seeming to be conventional is shattered in the end. Lennie's flaw grows into a potential for evil, and every evil is ascribed to him after his unwitting murder of Curley's wife. The objective image of the good life in the future, "a little house and a couple of acres an' a cow and some pigs," is opposed sharply to the present sordid reality of the bunkhouse and the ranch. Minor characters remain little more than opposed types, identifiable by allegorical tags. Curley is the unsure husband, opposed to and fearful of his sluttish, unnamed wife. Slim is a minor god in his perfect mastery of his work. His serenity is contrasted sharply with Curley's hysterical inability to please or to control his wife, and it contrasts as easily with the wife's constant, obvious discontent. Candy and Crooks are similar types, men without love. Both are abused by Curley, his wife, and the working crew. (Lennie might fall into this category of defenselessness, if he were aware enough to realize the situation; but he is not.) These sharp oppositions and typed personae restrict the development of the novel. The merely subordinate characters, such as Carlson and Whit, who only begin or fill out a few scenes, are strictly nonhuman, since they remain abstract instruments within a design.

The climax of that design is simplified in its turn, since it serves only to manipulate Lennie into a moral situation beyond his understanding. The climax is doubled, a pairing of opposites. In its first half, when Curley's wife attempts to seduce Lennie as a way to demonstrate her hatred of Curley, Lennie is content (in his nice innocence) to stroke her soft hair; but he is too violent, and he snaps her neck in a panic miscalculation as he tries to force her to be quiet. In the second half, George shoots Lennie to prevent a worse death at the hands of others. The melodramatic quality of these events will be considered at a later point. Here, it is more important to observe, in the design, that the climax pairs an exploration of the ambiguity of love in the rigid contrast between the different motives that activate Curley's wife and

George. Curley's wife wants to use Lennie to show her hatred for Curley; George shoots Lennie out of a real affection
for him. The attempted seduction balances the knowing
murder; both are disastrous expressions of love. Lennie is
the unknowing center of the design in both halves of this climax. Steinbeck's control is all too evident. There is not much
sense of dramatic illumination because the quality of the
paired climax is that of a mechanical problem of joining two
parallels. Lennie's necessary passivity enforces the quality
of a mechanical design. He is only the man to whom things
happen. Being so limited, he is incapable of providing that
sudden widening insight which alone justifies an artist's extreme dependence on a rigid design. Therefore, in general,
Of Mice and Men remains a simple anecdote.

It would be a mistake to conclude that the limited scope of
the materials is the only or the effective cause of the simplification. Writers frequently begin their work with anecdotal
materials. Most often, however, they expand the reference of
such materials through a knowing exercise of their medium.
It is Steinbeck's inability to exercise his medium or, perhaps
more fundamentally, to select a proper medium, which en-
sures the limited reference, the lack of a widening insight.

A THINNING OF MATERIALS

In his discussion of the play-novelette form in *Stage,* Steinbeck dismisses the objection that allegory is an overly limited form, but the objection is serious. *Of Mice and Men* is
not merely a brief novel. It is limited in what its structure
can make of its materials. Moreover, Steinbeck hoped to
achieve precisely that limitation ... although, it is true, he
felt the form would ensure a concentration, a focus, of the
materials. Instead, there is a deliberate thinning of materials
that are thin (or theatrical) to begin with.

In fact, Steinbeck uses every possible device to thin out
the effect of the materials. Foreshadowing is overworked.
Lennie's murder of Curley's wife is the catastrophe that
George has been dreading from the start. It is precisely the
fate that a fluffy animal like Curley's wife should meet at the
hands of Lennie, who has already killed mice and a puppy
with his overpowering tenderness. When Curley's wife
makes clear her intention to seduce the first available man
and the course of events abandons Lennie to her, the result
is inevitable. But that inevitability does not have tragic qual-

ities. The result is merely arranged, the characters merely inarticulate, and the action develops without illumination. Lennie can hardly distinguish between a dead pup and the dead woman:

> Lennie went back and looked at the dead girl. The puppy lay close to her. Lennie picked it up. "I'll throw him away," he said. "It's bad enough like it is."

The relative meaninglessness of his victims substitutes pathos for tragedy. Curley's rather shadowy wife underlines the substitution: She is characterless, nameless, and constantly discontent, so her death inspires none of the sympathy one might feel for a kind or a serene woman. Others respond to her death wholly in light of Lennie's predicament—from George's loving concern to Curley's blustering need for revenge—not his character. Everything that is excellent in the novel tends to relate, intensely if narrowly, to that emphasis. Within these limits, much that Steinbeck does is done excellently. The essential question is whether the treatment of the materials is intense enough to justify their evident manipulation, their narrowed pathos.

UNCONVENTIONAL MORALITY

The novel communicates most intensely a theme of unconventional morality. Lennie does commit murder, but he remains guiltless because he is not responsible for what he does. Yet the morality is only a statement of the pathos of Lennie's situation, not an exploration of guilt and innocence. A development through parallels and juxtapositions does little to expand the stated theme. Carlson parallels Lennie's violence on a conventional level when he insists on killing Candy's ancient, smelly dog. Carlson's reasoning is that the group has a right to wrong the individual. Lennie is incapable of any logic, even of this twisted sort, and he is never cruel by choice; that potential moral complexity is neglected in the design to permit the brutal simplicity of the group's response to Carlson's argument and to Lennie's crime. Carlson's crime is approved by the group: He abuses power to invade another man's desire for affection, reduced to a worthless dog. Lennie's crime is an accident in an attempt to express affection; murder is too serious for the group to ignore, so Lennie is hunted down. We are intended to notice the irony that Carlson's crime inverts Lennie's. That simple, paralleled irony substitutes for a possible, intense, necessarily complex, and ambiguous development of the materials. The rendered development, not the materials themselves, produces this simply mechanical irony.

Certainly the theme of unconventional morality offers tragic possibilities in a dimension beyond the anecdotal or the sketch of a character or event. From that viewpoint, the oppositions can expand into tragic awareness, at least potentially. They can even be listed, as follows. Lennie is good in his intentions, but evil in fact. The group is good in wanting to punish a murderer, but evil in misunderstanding that Lennie is guiltless. Counterwise, George, Candy, and Slim are endowed with understanding by their roles as the friend, the man without hope, and the god, but they are powerless against the group. Curley's wife is knowingly evil in exploiting Lennie's powerful body and weak mind. Curley is evil in exploiting all opportunities to prove his manhood. These two are pathetic in their human limitations, not tragic. George enacts an unconventional morality less by accident than any of the others. He feels strongly that, in being compelled to look after Lennie, he has given up the good times he might have had, but he knows the sacrifice is better, that he and Lennie represent an idealized variety of group-man. Slim's early, sympathetic insight makes this explicit:

> "You guys travel around together?" [Slim's] tone was friendly. It invited confidence without demanding it. "Sure," said George. "We kinda look after each other." He indicated Lennie with his thumb. "He ain't bright. Hell of a good worker, though. Hell of a nice fella, but he ain't bright. I've knew him for a long time." Slim looked through George and beyond him. "Ain't many guys travel around together," he mused. "I don't know why. Maybe ever'body in the whole damn world is scared of each other." "It's a lot nicer to go around with a guy you know," said George.

This important passage centers the theme of unconventional morality. It celebrates a relationship "the whole damn world" is incapable of imagining, given the ugly context of ranch life and sordid good times, and it locates the good life in friendship, not in the material image of the little farm. This passage is the heart of the novel.

But a novel cannot be structured solely on the basis of a theme, even a fundamental theme. Too much else must be simplified. Worse, the unconventional morality located in friendship produces Lennie's death, not only because Steinbeck can see no other way to conclude. Lennie dies necessarily because friendship can go no further than it does go, and nothing can be made of the dreamlike ideal of the little farm. The extreme simplification is that Steinbeck can do nothing with Lennie after he has been exhibited. These limitations derive from the simplification required by the play-novelette form. Steinbeck appears to be aware that formal limitations need some widening, since he imbeds Lennie's happiest and most intense consciousness of the good life of friends in an ironic context:

> George said, "Guys like us got no fambly. They make a little stake an' then they blow it in. They ain't got nobody in the worl' that gives a hoot in hell about 'em——" *"But not us,"* Lennie cried happily. "Tell about us now." George was quiet for a moment. "But not us," he said. "Because——" "Because I got you an'——" "An' I got you. We got each other, that's what, that gives a hoot in hell about us," Lennie cried in triumph.

The passage extends friendship beyond its boundary; it celebrates a species of marriage, minus the sexual element, between Lennie and George. But the content of the passage is qualified heavily by its position; George shoots Lennie after retelling the story about the little farm that always quiets Lennie. As further irony, precisely the responsibilities of a perfect friendship require George to shoot Lennie. The mob that would hang Lennie for murder is in the background throughout the scene. The situation is moving, but the effect is local. The ironies relate only to Lennie's pathetic situation; they do not aid an understanding of Lennie or account (beyond plot) for his death. . . .

An Abrupt Ending

Lennie's murder propels George into a sudden prominence that has no structural basis. Is the novel concerned with Lennie's innocence or George's guilt? The formal requirements of a play-novelette mandate a structural refocus. Steinbeck needs a high point to ring down the curtain. With Lennie dead, Steinbeck must use and emphasize George's guilt. The close is formulated—the result of a hasty switch—not structured from preceding events, so it produces an inconclusive ending in view of what has happened previously. And the ideal of the farm vanishes with Lennie's death, when George tells Candy the plan is off.

Here the difficulty is with a structure that requires a climax which cannot be achieved once Lennie, the center of the novel, is removed; but Lennie must be killed off when his existence raises problems of characterization more complex than the play-novelette form can express. Materials and structure pull against each other and finally collapse into an oversimplified conclusion that removes rather than faces the central theme.

The abrupt "solution" rests on melodrama, on sudden, purely plot devices of focus and refocus. Such overt manipulation indicates that in its practice the play-novelette is not a new form. Steinbeck's experience, his mature technical skill do not finally disguise his wish to return to his earliest fictional efforts to realize complex human behavior by way of an extreme simplification of structure and materials. His deliberate avoidance of an organic structure and his consequent dependence on a formula, on the exercise of technique within an artistic vacuum, exhausts the significance of the play-novelette theory. His practice, as in *Of Mice and Men,* does not lead to serious efforts and to a real achievement in the art of the novel. Rather, it leads to manipulations designed to effect a simplification of structure and materials. So much skill, directed toward so little, is disturbing. But the skill is absolutely there.

Chronology

1902
John Steinbeck born February 27

1903
Wright brothers' airplane flight

1906
San Francisco earthquake and fire

1909
Steinbeck's sister Mary born; Model T Ford first mass produced

1914
World War I begins in Europe; Panama Canal opens

1917
United States enters World War I

1919
Treaty of Versailles ending World War I; Steinbeck graduates from Salinas High School and enters Stanford University

1920
Steinbeck works on the Spreckels sugar ranch and gathers impressions about ranch life, which he will later fictionalize in *Of Mice and Men*

1925
Steinbeck goes to New York, working as a laborer and as a reporter for the *American* newspaper

1927
Charles Lindbergh's first solo transatlantic flight

1928
Talking pictures; first Mickey Mouse cartoon

1929

Stock market crash in America; Hoover becomes president; Steinbeck publishes *Cup of Gold*

1930

Steinbeck marries Carol Henning; meets Edward Ricketts in Pacific Grove, California

1932

America in Great Depression; Charles Lindbergh Jr. kidnapped and murdered; Steinbeck publishes *Pastures of Heaven*

1933

Franklin D. Roosevelt becomes president; Steinbeck publishes *To a God Unknown*

1934

Steinbeck wins O. Henry Prize for "The Murder"; mother dies

1935

Works Progress Administration, work relief for unemployed; Steinbeck publishes *Tortilla Flat*; wins Commonwealth Club of California Gold Medal; Pascal Covici becomes Steinbeck's publisher

1936

Steinbeck publishes *In Dubious Battle*; father dies; publishes articles on migrants in *San Francisco News*

1937

Steinbeck publishes *Of Mice and Men*; Theater Union in San Francisco performs *Of Mice and Men* from the book; stage version performed on Broadway and wins Drama Critics Circle Award; publishes *The Red Pony*, three parts

1938

Steinbeck publishes *The Long Valley* and *Their Blood Is Strong*, a pamphlet based on *Sun* articles about migrants

1939

World War II begins in Europe; Steinbeck publishes *The Grapes of Wrath*

1940

Steinbeck and Ricketts's research trip to the Sea of Cortez; Steinbeck wins Pulitzer Prize for *The Grapes of Wrath*; films "The Forgotten Village" in Mexico; film versions of *The Grapes of Wrath* and *Of Mice and Men*

1941

Japanese bomb Pearl Harbor; America enters World War II; Steinbeck publishes *Sea of Cortez* with Ricketts

1942

Steinbeck publishes *The Moon Is Down*; writes script for *Bombs Away;* Steinbeck and Carol Henning divorce; film version of *Tortilla Flat*

1943

Steinbeck marries Gwendolyn Conger; they move to New York; film version of *The Moon Is Down*

1944

D-day invasion of Normandy; Steinbeck writes script for *Lifeboat* with Alfred Hitchcock; son Thomas born

1945

Franklin D. Roosevelt dies; Harry Truman becomes president; Americans drop first atomic bomb on Hiroshima; World War II ends; Steinbeck publishes *Cannery Row*; *The Red Pony*, four parts; "The Pearl of the World" in *Woman's Home Companion*

1946

First meeting of the United Nations; son John born

1947

Steinbeck publishes *The Wayward Bus* and *The Pearl*

1948

Berlin blockade and airlift; Steinbeck publishes *A Russian Journal*; elected to American Academy of Letters; film version of *The Pearl*; Edward Ricketts dies; Steinbeck and Gwendolyn Conger divorce

1949

Film version of *The Red Pony*

1950

America involved in Korean War; Steinbeck publishes *Burning Bright*, novel and play; writes script for *Viva Zapata!*; marries Elaine Scott

1951

Steinbeck publishes *Log from the Sea of Cortez*

1952

Steinbeck publishes *East of Eden*

1953

Dwight D. Eisenhower becomes president

1954

Steinbeck publishes *Sweet Thursday*

1955

Civil rights movement begins; film version of *East of Eden*

1957

Steinbeck publishes *The Short Reign of Pippin IV*; film version of *The Wayward Bus*

1958

Steinbeck publishes *Once There Was a War*

1959

Alaska admitted as forty-ninth state; Hawaii admitted as fiftieth

1960

Steinbeck tours America with dog Charley

1961

John F. Kennedy becomes president; Soviets put up Berlin Wall; first U.S. manned suborbital flight; Steinbeck publishes *The Winter of Our Discontent*

1962

Cuban missile crisis; Steinbeck publishes *Travels with Charley in Search of America*; awarded Nobel Prize in literature

1963

John F. Kennedy assassinated; Lyndon Johnson becomes president

1964–1975

America involved in Vietnam War

1964

Steinbeck awarded the Presidential Medal of Freedom

1965

Steinbeck reports from Vietnam for *Newsday*

1966

Steinbeck publishes *America and Americans*

1968

Martin Luther King Jr. assassinated; televised versions of *Travels with Charley*, *Of Mice and Men*, and *The Grapes of Wrath*; Steinbeck dies on December 20; buried in Salinas

1969

Richard M. Nixon becomes president; publication of *Journal of a Novel: The* East of Eden *Letters*

1970

Opera version of *Of Mice and Men*

1975

Steinbeck: A Life in Letters, edited by Elaine Steinbeck and Robert Wallstein; publication of *The Acts of King Arthur and His Noble Knights*, Steinbeck's unfinished translation of *Le Morte Darthur*

1981

New televised version of *Of Mice and Men*

1992

New film version of *Of Mice and Men*

FOR FURTHER RESEARCH

ABOUT JOHN STEINBECK

Richard Astro, *John Steinbeck and Edward F. Ricketts: The Shaping of a Novelist.* Minneapolis: University of Minnesota Press, 1973.

Jackson J. Benson, *Looking for Steinbeck's Ghost.* Norman: University of Oklahoma Press, 1988.

———, *The True Adventures of John Steinbeck, Writer.* New York: Viking Press, 1984.

Robert Murray Davis, ed., *Steinbeck: A Collection of Critical Essays.* Englewood Cliffs, NJ: Prentice-Hall, 1942.

John Ditsky, *John Steinbeck: Life, Work, and Criticism.* Fredericton, N.B., Canada: York, 1985.

Thomas Fensch, *Steinbeck and Covici: The Story of a Friendship.* Middlebury, VT: Paul S. Ericksson, 1979.

Joseph Fontenrose, *John Steinbeck: An Introduction and Interpretation.* New York: Barnes and Noble, 1963.

Warren French, *John Steinbeck.* New York: Twayne Publishers, 1961.

James Gray, *John Steinbeck* (pamphlet). Minneapolis: University of Minnesota Press, 1971.

Charlotte Cook Hadella, *Of Mice and Men: A Kinship of Powerlessness.* New York: Twayne Publishers, 1995.

Tetsumaro Hayashi, ed., *Steinbeck and the Arthurian Theme.* Steinbeck Monograph Series, no. 5, 1975. Muncie: Steinbeck Society of America, Ball State University, 1975.

———, *A Study Guide to John Steinbeck: A Handbook to His Major Works.* Metuchen, NJ: Scarecrow Press, 1974.

Sunita Jain, *John Steinbeck's Concept of Man: A Critical Study of His Novels.* New Delhi: New Statesman, 1979.

Thomas Kiernan, *The Intricate Music: A Biography of John Steinbeck.* Boston: Little, Brown, 1979.

Howard Levant, *The Novels of John Steinbeck: A Critical Study.* Columbia: University of Missouri Press, 1974.

Peter Lisca, *John Steinbeck: Nature and Myth.* New York: Crowell, 1978.

———, *The Wide World of John Steinbeck.* New Brunswick, NJ: Rutgers University Press, 1958.

Lester J. Marks, *Thematic Design in the Novels of John Steinbeck.* The Hague: Mouton, 1969.

Joseph R. Millichap, *Steinbeck and Film.* New York: Ungar, 1983.

Harry Thornton Moore, *The Novels of John Steinbeck: A First Critical Study.* Chicago: Normandie House, 1939.

Louis Owens, *John Steinbeck's Re-Vision of America.* Athens: University of Georgia Press, 1985.

Elaine Steinbeck and Robert Wallsten, *Steinbeck: A Life in Letters.* New York: Viking Press, 1975.

Brian St. Pierre, *John Steinbeck: The California Years.* San Francisco: Chronicle Books, 1983.

E.W. Tedlock Jr. and C.V. Wicker, eds., *Steinbeck and His Critics: A Record of Twenty-Five Years.* Albuquerque: University of New Mexico Press, 1957.

HISTORICAL AND LITERARY BACKGROUND

Frederick Lewis Allen, *Since Yesterday: The Nineteen-Thirties in America, September 3, 1929–September 3, 1939.* New York: Harper & Brothers, 1940.

Fon Boardman Jr., *The Thirties: America and the Great Depression.* New York: Henry Z. Walck, 1967.

Cletus E. Daniel, *Bitter Harvest: A History of California Farmworkers, 1870–1941.* Berkeley: University of California Press, 1982.

William Dudley, ed., *The Great Depression.* San Diego: Greenhaven Press, 1994.

Winifred L. Dusenbury, *The Theme of Loneliness in Modern American Drama.* Gainesville: University of Florida Press, 1960.

Maxwell Geismar, *Writers in Crisis: The American Novel, 1925–1945.* Boston: Houghton Mifflin, 1942.

Robert Goldston, *The Great Depression: The United States in the Thirties.* Indianapolis: Bobbs-Merrill, 1968.

Frederick J. Hoffman, *The Modern Novel in America.* Chicago: Henry Regnery, 1951.

Leonard Lutwack, *Heroic Fiction: The Epic Tradition and American Novels of the Twentieth Century.* Carbondale: Southern Illinois University Press, 1971.

Studs Terkel, *Hard Times: An Oral History of the Great Depression.* New York: Pantheon Books, 1970.

Edmund Wilson, *The Boys in the Back Room: Notes on California Novelists.* San Francisco: Colt Press, 1941.

WORKS BY JOHN STEINBECK

Cup of Gold (1929)

Pastures of Heaven (1932)

To a God Unknown (1933)

Tortilla Flat (1935)

In Dubious Battle (1936)

"The Harvest Gypsies," published in *San Francisco News* (1936)

Saint Katie the Virgin (1936)

Of Mice and Men (1937)

The Red Pony, three parts (1937)

The Long Valley (1938)

Their Blood Is Strong, pamphlet of *San Francisco News* articles (1938)

The Grapes of Wrath (1939)

The Forgotten Village, a film (1940)

Film versions of *The Grapes of Wrath* and *Of Mice and Men* (1940)

Sea of Cortez, with Edward F. Ricketts (1941)

The Moon Is Down, novel and play (1942)

Bombs Away (1942)

Film version of *Tortilla Flat* (1942)

Film version of *The Moon Is Down* (1943)

Script for *Lifeboat*, a film (1944)

Cannery Row (1945)

The Red Pony, four parts (1945)

"The Pearl of the World" in *Woman's Home Companion* (1945)

The Wayward Bus (1947)

The Pearl (1947)

A Russian Journal (1948)

Film version of *The Pearl* (1948)

Film version of *The Red Pony* (1949)

Burning Bright, novel and play (1950)

Script for *Viva Zapata!*, a film (1950)

Log from the Sea of Cortez (1951)

East of Eden (1952)

Sweet Thursday (1954)

Pipe Dream, a musical based on *Sweet Thursday* (1955)

Film version of *East of Eden* (1955)

The Short Reign of Pippin IV (1957)

Film version of *The Wayward Bus* (1957)

Once There Was a War (1958)

The Winter of Our Discontent (1961)

Travels with Charley in Search of America (1962)

Newsday columns (1965)

America and Americans (1966)

Television versions of *Travels with Charley, Of Mice and Men,* and *The Grapes of Wrath*; "Here's Where I Belong," a musical (1968)

Journal of a Novel: The East of Eden *Letters* (1969)

Opera version of *Of Mice and Men* (1970)

The Acts of King Arthur and His Noble Knights (1973)

Steinbeck: A Life in Letters, edited by Elaine Steinbeck and Robert Wallstein (1975)

INDEX